D0017646

Never Call Them Jerks

Healthy Responses to Difficult Behavior

Arthur Paul Boers

Foreword by
David W. Augsburger

An Alban Institute Publication

Scripture quotations unless otherwise noted are from the New Revised Standard Version of the Bible, copyright © 1989, Division of Christian Education of the National Council of the Churches of Christ in the United States of America, and are used by permission.

Copyright © 1999 by the Alban Institute. All rights reserved.

This material may not be photocopied or reproduced in any way without written permission.

Library of Congress Card Number 99-73550
ISBN 1-56699-218-4

CONTENTS

Arthur Boers was a difficult student during his first years at seminary—and he was majoring in "Peace Studies," no less! One faculty member had a choice of two diagnostic labels for him. Another had two alternate careers to suggest. To make matters worse, he was extremely bright, often passionate, and on the particular issue in conflict, obviously right. His training in social analysis, his deep concern for justice, his willingness to get embroiled in tough situations, and his persistent staying power disturbed the surface layers of the Mennonite social contract which views community as *niceness* (denial), as *forbearance* (avoidance), as *considerateness* (distancing). Beneath these deceptive qualities, of course, the community was connected by the resilient sinews of stubborn loyalty to an Anabaptist struggle for faithful integrity in our life together. Art wanted to get to these deeper levels more quickly, and without some of the usual social niceties.

He troubled the waters. Such "angels" are immediately recognized as "troublesome" people and labeled as "troubled." The pool of Bethesda in John 5:1-15 comes to mind as an apt metaphor for his effect on our community. "When the calm waters are stirred, those who get wet get healed," someone said. Indeed, this shake-up helped us all grow a little. As we watched Art graduate, we wondered what other waters he might agitate, aware that his mark on our community had been good and would prove to be so elsewhere as well.

Arthur Boers has the gifts for being there when conflicts happen, for bringing issues that we consent to leave invisible into the clear, reasonable light, and for joining in the struggle for a new justice. In *Never Call Them Jerks*, he displays these gifts again: He allows us to walk with him in the process of maintaining a core of calm while we examine the whole system of a church in pain. It's easier to give in to our anxiety and single out a particular point of friction as constituting the whole problem. This paranoid temptation is a part of the childhood layer of every person's developmental track ("He started it, she caused it, it's all his fault, the rest of us are innocent, ok?") and lies just under the surface of every community where people join their slowly maturing social skills. When tensions rise, the impulse to finger the foe and exclude the troublemaker is instant, powerful, and often logical in its either/or, all-or-nothing clarity.

"True Christian community is found in the place where the person you like least to be with always is," or so Dietrich Bonhoeffer argued. "When that person dies or moves away, a worse one always appears to take the empty place," a Quaker friend has added. "It's not the person that's the problem anyway," Speed Leas notes. "It is the system that creates a gadfly role and appoints someone to fill it." Better the problem person whom we know than the understudy whom we don't know standing in the wings waiting to assume the role of troublemaker.

Arthur Boers demonstrates here that he understands Martin Buber's helpful categories of community; namely, that authentic Christian community is not a "community of similarity," a union of like-minded people who have eluded or eliminated all potential detractors. Instead, it is a "community of diversity" that does not exclude the intrinsic and natural variation and divergence that constitutes human groupings.

Community, when it is faithful in welcoming its actual members, contains (brace yourself!)

- contrasts in perspective
- tensions in relationships
- ambivalence in motivations
- variety in preferences
- diversity in values
- competition for resources
- complexities of human needs
- toxicity in personalities
- immaturity in development

—all held together by implicit and explicit contracts, covenants, and the conversations that keep them alive. When something goes wrong—whether it be in the interpersonal connections, the balance of influences, the distribution of power in its many currencies, or the pattern and flow of communication—

conflict then appears as a warning signal that something is about to mal-function and someone somewhere is already feeling pain.

Shooting the messenger, blaming the one who shouts "fire" for being the arsonist, or excluding those who are willing to speak up only buries the injury for the moment and contributes to the creation of later and greater injustices. The appearance in recent years of a series of books on dealing with "difficult" or "impossible" people has only furthered this primitive practice of "defining people of the lie" or "naming disruptive and destructive person-alities." This book, by a practicing pastor and consultant, stands firmly out-side such linear cause-and-effect explanations and nudges us toward look-ing to the whole, exploring the larger picture, charting the way the system is functioning, and making changes in the whole (the epilogue alone is worth the price of the book).

As I absorbed Art's words, I found myself comparing his insights with those scant learnings I have accumulated from several decades of consult-ing with churches in open conflict. I share them here as the true foreword to this book—a word before the real monograph like an *hors d'ouevre* before the *plate du jour*—to whet your appetite for the banquet to follow (though be warned: there will be servings of some tough joints, humble pie, and more).

Systemic learnings is short form:

- When I observe a fault in you that rankles me and evokes in me an immediate label to explain our differences—then I have reason to sus-pect that the fault I see in you is in me too. *(My immediate inner argument with this statement is significant evidence of its possible truth.)*
- There is no such thing as resistance in the pastoral counseling or pasto-ral care relationship; there is only my inability to see the situation fully from the other's perspective or my unwillingness to recognize their right to say no. *(My resistance to this conclusion suggests that I do not fully see how it applies to my last "difficult" counselee or my most recent "painful" conflict.)*
- There are no communal conflicts with a single cause, a solitary villain, or an evil person who must be named, neutralized, neutered, or nuked. *(But any community in conflict is much relieved by the simple act of identifying a scapegoat and loading the blame on its head.)*
- When the temptation to label, finger, blame—or its reverse side, to excuse, exonerate, defend—becomes more attractive than exploring

the whole, I will whisper to myself, "It's the system, stupid." *(Lasting change is system change. Lingering healing is communal growth. Effective pastoring pastors the system as well as the participants, the body as well as the organs and appendages.)*

- Labeling, diagnosing, defining discrete linear causes in a conflict situation is a kind of nominalism that loves the Bible more than its central figure, the proposition more than the one who proposes, the menu more than the meal.

Enough of the menu. Let's get on with the real meal, served with uncommon art.

David W. Augsburger
Professor of Pastoral Care and Counseling
Fuller Theological Seminary, Pasadena, California

ACKNOWLEDGMENTS

This grows from the intersection of my ministry, personal growth, and spirituality. I am privileged to keep company with many exceptional colleagues. I am grateful to my Day Away group: Tom Cullen, Ross Macdonald, Peter Roebbelen, and to Ruth Anderson and her late husband, Hugh, who provided gracious and hospitable space for us. I am also indebted to the Prayer Accountability group: David Martin, Mary Schiedel, and Sue Steiner. I dare not imagine where I might be without these folk helping me keep centered and accountable.

Along the way I appreciated support received from other peers, including Donald Bardwell, Muriel Bechtel, Jim Brown, Edwin Epp, Anna Hemmendinger, the late Vernon Leis, Allan Rudy-Froese, Mary Mae Schwartzentruber, Eleanor Snyder, Dave Tiessen, Darrel Toews, and Rebecca and Tom Yoder Neufeld. I am proud to count myself in their company.

I am grateful for mentors in ministry along the way: Herb Schultz, who taught me a lot during some of the hardest moments of my life; Henri Nouwen, who ministered to me in several crises and whom I eventually considered a spiritual father; Doris Gascho, who helped me grow as a minister; Peter L. VanKatwyk, who more than anyone else taught and showed me how to apply family systems in life and ministry; Arnie Weigel, who (along with Doris and Peter) helped me with earlier work on this book's subject; and Marcus Smucker, who has long been one of my key mentors. Thank you all.

I also appreciate the spiritual support of and connection with Abbot Andrew Marr and the monks at St. Gregory's Abbey, Three Rivers, Michigan, where I am an oblate and where I have found a spiritual shelter and home for almost two decades.

Each church I have served as a pastor has been a privilege. I owe a special debt of gratitude to Bloomingdale Mennonite Church, Bloomingdale, Ontario, where I have served the longest, have had the most opportunity to deal with difficult behavior (my own and others'), and have been given space, freedom, and wholehearted encouragement to serve, study, write, pray, exercise my gifts, and grow as a person and a minister.

I am grateful for Alban's good work over the years, helping church leaders learn all the things we did not learn or could not take in at seminary. Thus I am pleased for the Alban Institute's work with this book and particularly for the gracious and supportive work of my editor, David Lott.

Over the years, I have been especially privileged to blend my interest in writing with my commitment to excellence in ministry through collaboration with *The Christian Ministry*. Special thanks are due to Victoria A. Rebeck, the *Ministry*'s managing editor, who has become my friend along the way.

While all of those mentioned above supported me in key ways at various and many points, my family has been the most important element in my growth, ministry, and being at all times. So a huge "Thank you!" to my dear wife Lorna McDougall, and our two God-given offspring, Erin and Paul.

I am greatly blessed and immensely grateful!

INTRODUCTION

*No wild beasts are so cruel as the Christians in their dealings
with each other.*
  —Ammianus Marcellinus (Roman historian, c. A.D. 330-395)

A pastor sat down beside me at the funeral of a colleague who had been an
important mentor to us. My pewmate and I had been acquainted long enough
for respect and even affection to have developed between us. She is an
exemplary pastor.

Having arrived early for the service, we began talking. She confided a
devastating experience that she had endured as a pastor several years ago.
The conflict and its aftermath still hurt as she spoke of it. I was surprised
for several reasons. I had no idea of the conflict. I knew of her good work
and could not imagine such difficulties for her. And in my experience pastors generally do not talk about "such things."

I was saddened that she felt isolated. But she is not alone. Some suggest that the difficult behavior in congregations that contributes to pastoral
terminations is often deliberately overlooked, a "dirty little secret." A terminated pastor writes:

> Of the myriad church problems receiving media attention these
> days—from mainline membership losses to incidents of sexual
> abuse—there is one that has remained largely in the ecclesiastical
> closet. Local churches, denominational officials and clergy all help
> perpetuate this problem by being [loath] to acknowledge it. The
> former two find that ignoring it is easier than rooting out its causes,
> and the latter want to avoid a painful issue that may carry a pro-
> fessional stigma.[1]

On the basis of his experience and many conversations with other terminated pastors, the author concludes that "churches and denominations are covering up a widespread pattern of destructive behavior." I do not buy the charge of a "cover-up," but I do find that people often regard these issues as difficult and perhaps even distasteful to discuss.

I am concerned about "cover-up" charges because ministers, as hard as our work may be, are often tempted to play "pity-me" or "blame-them" games about the way others treat us. While we cannot control how others treat us, as responsible leaders we can decide how to respond. I am concerned with what it means to exercise responsible leadership in the face of behavior we find difficult.

Conflict in the Church

These concerns are part of a larger issue, church conflict. Conflict in the church often surprises us. Occasionally those most surprised are pastors themselves. Some enter ministry with naïve idealism and are caught off guard by the vehemence of church conflicts. They feel wounded when they are the focus of such behavior. Yet conflict in the church should not surprise us. In church, emotional issues are close to the surface. Worship ceremonies, small-group experiences, and pastoral care often bring denied, hidden, submerged, or repressed feelings to the surface. Little wonder that matters may explode in unexpected ways.

One issue in church conflict is dealing with the difficult, destructive, and aggressive behavior of some. This challenge is one for which many pastors and church leaders, especially those with little life experience, are ill-prepared.

Pastors sometimes complain that seminary training did not prepare them for practical challenges. Perhaps we *were* taught but were simply unable to hear. My lack of experience certainly precluded me from understanding many church conflicts. I have gone back and read some seminary texts and feel that only now do I understand them.

Dealing with Difficult Behavior

Although many do not know how to respond, they recognize that a problem exists. When I tell people that I am writing on "difficult behavior in the congregation," I am often met with smirks. Many know of such phenomena and immediately grasp some of the concerns involved. In some resources that treat these issues, individuals who manifest difficult behavior are variously referred to as "well-intentioned dragons," "antagonists in the church," "alligators," "troublesome people," or "clergy killers." One colleague refers euphemistically to "very challenging persons" or "VCPs."

Some believe that difficult behavior or gross incivility in church, especially toward pastors, is worsening. The aforementioned terminated pastor speaks of a "proliferation of congregational conflicts in which the pastor is the target," calling this trend a "hidden crisis." Several years ago Rabbi Edwin Friedman, a family-systems therapist, also observed an "extraordinary increase in church and synagogue upheavals during the past twenty years."[2] Forced exits are often closely related to the difficult behavior of parishioners. In 1996, *Leadership* magazine conducted a national survey of Protestant pastors: 23 percent claimed to "have been fired at least once, and 43 percent said a 'faction' (less than ten people) forced them out."[3] If such reports are true, then the cost of church conflicts in general and difficult behavior within the church in particular is high.

What is "Difficult Behavior?"

Experts differ in their understandings of what constitutes difficult behavior and their approaches to what should be done about it. Speed Leas, a church conflict-resolution specialist, describes five levels of church conflict: (I) problems to solve, (II) disagreement, (III) contest, (IV) fight/flight, and (V) intractable situations.[4] We consider difficult behavior to include any kind of distorted, adversarial, or uncivil behavior found in what Leas terms Level III, IV, or V conflicts.

The first two levels are not relevant here. At Level III (contest) people work for win/lose solutions. Factions often form, and the language becomes more intense. At Level IV (fight/flight), contestants attempt to damage or oust each other. Level V (intractable) is unmanageable, reflecting conflict gone out of control. Here, says Leas, parties try to destroy each other, metaphorically if not literally.

At Level V parties usually perceive themselves as part of an eternal cause, fighting for universal principles. Since the ends are all-important, they believe they are compelled to continue to fight; they cannot stop. Indeed, the costs to society, truth and God of withdrawal from the fight are perceived as greater than the costs of defeating the others even through prolonged conflict. Therefore, continuing the fight is the only choice; one cannot choose to stop fighting.

Leas shows that at Level III (contest) one begins encountering key distortions of thinking that grow worse as conflict escalates:

- Magnification (seeing oneself as more benevolent and the opponent as more malevolent than is the case).
- Dichotomization (dualistic thinking that sharply divides us and them, right and wrong, fight and flight).
- Overgeneralization ("always," "never," "everybody," "nobody" language).
- Assumption (believing one can read the other's mind and motives).

Leas also cites a longer list of distorted thinking developed by rational-emotive therapists David S. Goodman and Maxie C. Maultsby, Jr.: being inconsistent and applying double standards, using non sequiturs, generalizing, exaggerating, building a case, shifting responsibility, viewing feelings as facts, perceiving memories as present-day realities, seeing distant possibilities as likely probabilities, imposing one's own "shoulds" on others, expecting rapid change, being stuck in established patterns, attributing responsibility for one's behavior to an external cause, assuming all responsibility for what happens, practicing perfectionism, and using magical thinking.

"Difficult behavior" is not conflict, criticism, argument, or occasional irrationality, all of which leaders can expect as a normal part of our work. "Difficult behavior" is not that which "pushes one's buttons." After all, people react variously to vastly different circumstances, as temperament and personality inventories show. We all have different "buttons."

"Difficult behavior" is patterned and sustained behavior that is abusive, irrational, hostile, adversarial, or distorted. It reflects the kinds of problematic behavior and distorted thinking enumerated in the Level III through V categories of conflict.

Overview

Church leadership demands responsibility in the face of difficult behavior. This book takes a family-systems approach. By adopting a "research stance" toward congregations and parishioners, church leaders increase their sense of control over self and their reactions, reduce their anxiety (and the anxiety of their system), and become less apt to overreact and thus more likely to challenge those with the most growth potential. Emotionally intelligent church leaders care for themselves, practice self-awareness, manage their emotions, observe and respect others' emotions, and handle relationships well. Responsible church leaders serve as models of a firm and assertive approach to conflict that is flexible but not floppy, compassionate but not "sloppy agape," steady but not immovable.

This book has a passion for church leaders who struggle with responding appropriately to difficult behavior, but it also has a passionate *pastoral* concern for any who may engage in difficult behavior.

Chapter 1 looks at what other authors say about dealing with difficult behavior. Most sources rely heavily on labeling and blaming. The focus of this book is not difficult people but the question of how church leaders can understand, respond to, and deal with difficult relationships and behavior.

Chapter 2's broader understanding of the dynamics of anxiety-provoking behavior gives us distance and helps us respond rather than react. This chapter applies family-systems theory to congregations. Seeing churches as wholistic, relational units; looking at multiple causation and interdependence; considering the influence of the family of origin; reflecting on the dynamics of stability and change; looking at multigenerational patterns; and examining triangulation—all these offer helpful perspectives on understanding difficult behavior and clues to how to respond. Symptoms of difficult behavior may not be directly resolvable or manageable. Systems thinking encourages us to look at symptoms as signs of problems below the surface. Then we can respond to those dynamics instead.

Chapter 3 examines hazards that contribute to difficult behavior in the congregation, including transference, countertransference, projection, symbolic role, pastoral idealism, chronic anxiety, and social incompetence. By tapping into various resources, the responsible leader grasps many "handles" for understanding difficult behavior. One who approaches difficult behavior from a "research stance" can respond with caution and poise. This attitude helps us to have compassion for those who manifest difficult behavior, urges us to be self-aware, and gives further clues about dealing responsibly with difficult behavior.

Chapter 4 considers unhealthy responses to difficult behavior. One such response is the retributive, hostile power play, or counterattack. Difficult behavior should not be resisted with difficult behavior. Many self-help books on difficult behavior recommend outwitting, subverting, outmaneuvering, or silencing opponents. But "hardball" is reactive. Forcing change usually does not work.

A bigger temptation in congregations is "softball" behavior: being indirect, passive, placating, nonconfrontational, sentimental, or appeasing. Such responses seem the opposite of "hardball," but they also are problematic and unhealthy. They show an inability to deal with the anxiety that differences, division, and differentiation provoke.

Finally, we ask why churches settle so easily into one unhealthy response or the other. It is important that leaders learn new or "adaptive" responses to challenges.

Chapter 5 suggests what *healthy* things congregations can do. Leaders help groups find direction. As congregations wrestle with difficult behavior, they need responsible leaders to counsel them on discovering the best responses. Leaders encourage maturity of response in the systems they lead, even though they realize that such goals may never be achieved.

We need healthy understandings of reconciliation and confrontation. Christian assertiveness does not give up or give in, balances respect of self and others, and shares goals for the common good. When faced with difficult behavior, leaders need to assess the church's health. This chapter discusses dealing with difficult behavior as it occurs at different levels of conflict. It also considers norms, both healthy and unhealthy, that groups may bring to conflicts. It also makes suggestions about "fair fighting."

Chapter 6 continues to examine the challenge of training churches in healthy ways of dealing with conflict: focusing on health and strength rather than on weakness and sabotage. Responsible leaders make every effort to lead congregations in becoming less anxious and more savvy in dealing with challenges. Other matters are also addressed—for example, the importance of using grievance procedures, expecting sabotage and dealing with it, and applying Matthew 18, today. Congregations can be urged to practice responsible assertiveness.

The most important challenge remains: determining what responsible leadership requires. That is the task of chapter 7 and following. While it is important to consider healthy congregational responses, it is most important to scrutinize the responsibilities of leaders. Many churches either do not know how to respond to destructive behavior or are incapable of doing so. Thus pastors are on the front line, and our responses are crucial.

Chapter 7 examines differentiation, the key to responsible leadership. To be differentiated is to know (and act on) one's own mind, especially when one's position differs from the group's. It requires staying in touch, taking nonreactive stands, and learning to deal with sabotage. This approach includes being a nonanxious presence, increasing toleration of pain and anxiety, dealing with triangulation, and facing fear.

Chapter 8 encourages leaders to face tough situations, "fierce landscapes," as places of challenge and growth. Leaders learn to deal with anxiety and to increase their threshold for pain. They deal with the anxiety of triangulation and the hazards of defensiveness. In dealing with criticism (turning critics into teachers) and learning to give criticism, we discover that difficult behavior presents an opportunity.

Chapter 9 addresses the essentials of attending to, focusing on, and taking care of ourselves. This self-care entails being focused on ourselves, not on "enemies." It demands self-examination and self-awareness. It means being savvy about danger signs but checking our perceptions. It requires attending to our relationship with God.

Throughout this book, you will find stories—some hopeful, some provocative. All are meant to teach, to inspire, and even occasionally to amuse.

Motivations

Attending an annual event for ministers, I was struck by the missing faces of companions who had attended previously. Several, because of bitter conflict in their congregational assignments, are no longer parish pastors. Some have even left the church. So broken and devastated were they by church conflicts that some lost their faith, or at least their willingness to be connected to the Christian community.

We cannot overestimate the spiritual havoc wreaked by bitter church conflicts and the cost of difficult behavior focused destructively on leaders. I looked at the pastors present at this latest event, aware that some were even then being hurt or ground up, and wondered which colleague would next disappear as "missing in action."

While I write out of collegial concern, a personal side informs this endeavor. I have been involved in devastating church conflicts. During one, I despaired, felt defeated, lost hope, and wondered whether I had made a mistake in becoming a pastor. As I shared my concerns with other pastors or told them horror stories of the behavior I had encountered, some commented to the effect: "Someday, you can write a book about this." That was no comfort! I had no intention of writing a book: The conflict was too painful. The difficulties seemed too high a price to pay for the sake of finding a writing project.

Yet here I am, years later, having written a book on this very subject. But I was not able to write it until I had wrestled with deep issues about my own leadership style, my own reactivity, my own spirituality, my own family of origin—all as part of becoming a responsible leader. The process has proved therapeutic and has brought me healing. And I have learned what it means to be a responsible leader in trying circumstances.

I hope that this book will alert many church leaders to possible problems, recurrent patterns, and common pitfalls. Like many authors, I will feel richly rewarded if this book helps just one reader through a difficult situation.

CHAPTER 1

Naming, Blaming, and Shaming Games

What do you do when you are faced with a new challenge? I go to some of my favorite places—libraries or bookstores—looking sometimes for entertainment, sometimes for escape, and sometimes for a specific resource about the problem I face.

Reading has proved for me to be good therapy and spiritual direction. Later I shall consider other ways and resources for dealing with concerns about difficult behavior, but for now we will look at some of the literature that is available. Alas, on the whole, there are few resources that are not problematic in one way or another.

Looking at the Resources

On the challenges of difficult behavior, one finds chiefly two kinds of books—general self-help books and books that examine church contexts.

Your local bookstore may have on its shelves general self-help books that begin to address the subject at hand. Often these are particularly directed to business or employment settings. While sometimes helpful, they usually label and categorize people indiscriminately. (Several are listed in the bibliography.) Here you might find ways of dealing with "hostile-aggressives," "complainers," "silent unresponsives," "super-agreeables," "negativists," "know-it-alls," or "indecisives." On the positive side, such books often point out that each person has the responsibility of deciding how to respond to difficult people. The authors recognize that while we cannot control or change others, we can take responsibility for our own actions, attitudes, and behavior.

Even so, most general self-help books offer diagnoses that are unhelpful at best and severely problematic at worst. They engage in blaming and finger-pointing and suggest courses of action that would tend to intensify the heat of conflict. They show little psychological insight, especially with their simplistic, pejorative, and negative labeling.

* * * * *

Not only general and secular self-help books indulge in labeling and diagnosing in response to difficult behavior. Three kinds of books deal with church contexts.

1. *General Approaches*: Some resources paint difficult behavior in the church with a broad brush. They contain nuggets of good advice but often adopt a general, anxious, and mistrustful tone, as evidenced in their use of broad and negative labeling: "clergy killers," "antagonists," "well-intentioned dragons," and "problem people."

I find such books too sweeping. They tend to advocate broad policies to fit a wide array of circumstances, with little sense of particular contexts and no appreciation for more extensive understandings of how churches function. Some even speak blithely of evil and the need for exorcisms.

Such general approaches can contribute to anxious mistrust when, as we shall see, one of our major goals is to reduce anxiety in both ourselves and in the emotional systems wherein they operate. Thus these resources can be counterproductive, bringing to mind the old nasty joke: "There are no problems in this church that a few Christian funerals wouldn't resolve." The Ananaias and Sapphira story (Acts 5), in which two parishioners are struck dead during a conflicted encounter with Peter, seems like an apt metaphor for these approaches.

2. *Detailing and Labeling Types of Antagonists*: Pastoral-leadership scholar Robert D. Dale's *Surviving Difficult Church Members* categorizes difficult people and offers advice for dealing with cliques, "crazymakers," sensitive Christians, hostile people, apathetic members, and traditionalists. He reminds us that we leaders are often difficult and have much to learn about ourselves from those whom we consider "difficult." He urges self-examination amid difficult circumstances, but I find his "survival" terminology and tendency toward labels unhelpful, even if his approach is less blatantly mistrustful than those described above.

3. *Diagnostic Understandings of Difficult Behavior in the Church*: A new member was appointed to the church council. Many complained

that she was "so negative" and "such a pessimist" that she could not make a good contribution. To their surprise, she turned out to be one of the hardest-working, most dedicated team players. This outcome reminded me to be cautious whenever I am tempted to label or diagnose people in church.

Yet several resources responsibly attempt to diagnose the personality dynamics and mental-health issues that underlie certain difficult behaviors in the church.

The most helpful author is Wayne E. Oates, an important voice in pastoral counseling and care. His most in-depth treatment is *Behind the Masks,* in which he deals with personality disorders and their connection to religious behavior. He gives attention to certain personality disorders as understood in *DSM-III (The Diagnostic and Statistical Manual of Mental Disorders,* third edition—the American Psychiatric Association's compilation of its systems of psychiatric diagnosis). While this discussion is helpful, the problem is that most pastors are not professionally or ethically qualified to diagnose.

A lighter book for pastoral caregivers is Oates's *The Care of Troublesome People* (the most positive title in the literature). Employing family-systems thinking, Oates gives counsel on dealing pastorally with the circumferential ("backbiting"), authoritarian ("power-driven"), competitive ("self-serving"), dependent ("clinging vine"), and soloist ("star performer"). Here he comes closest to labeling.

Conrad W. Weiser, psychologist and consultant on congregational matters, turns the tables on this discussion in *Healers–Harmed and Harmful.* Pastors can also suffer personality disorders and behave inappropriately and damage others, at times catastrophically so. Weiser deals with narcissism, woundedness, defensive structures, distortions in perception, depression, dependency, compulsivity, borderline behavior, transference, and countertransference. His approach is a needed counterbalance to some leaders' propensity to label and diagnose others. Our first professional obligation is to understand ourselves; without that understanding we are incapable of working with others in healthy or healing ways.

One other book diagnostically interprets difficult behavior in church. In *Understanding Anger in the Church*, pastoral-care expert Daniel Bagby helpfully explores anger and its relationship to the following problems and behaviors: depression, outspokenness, fear, numbness, manipulation, and withdrawal. Bagby offers a sensitive, sensible, and calm treatment of subjects that are inclined to raise the anxiety of pastors and parishioners alike. He emphasizes understanding and responding appropriately.

Most literature that deals with difficult behavior in the church relies to some extent on labels or diagnoses. Some, notably Oates and Bagby, offer diagnoses responsibly and with reliance on reputable psychological resources. Nevertheless, we must give some thought to the appropriateness of relying on labeling and diagnosing.

Limitations of Diagnoses and Labels

In an English school, a computer mistakenly labeled "bright" children as "intellectually challenged" and vice versa. Teachers treated the students accordingly. When bright children were treated as "challenged," their IQs declined, while "challenged" children treated as bright showed a rise in IQ.[1]

Reasons abound for questioning the helpfulness or appropriateness of labels and diagnoses. I admit that I sometimes find the labeling of self-help books amusing, especially when I am in a cynical frame of mind. Nonetheless, I recommend against such indulgence for these reasons:

1. *Labeling is itself difficult behavior*. Labeling falls into the kinds of uncivil behavior that we find in Level III to IV conflicts (in Speed Leas's system, described in the introduction), in which people use whatever means available to damage, oust, or destroy one another. In fact, labeling can reflect the distorted thinking that Leas enumerates: magnification, dichotomization, overgeneralization, exaggeration, and shifts of responsibility. By indulging in such labeling we ourselves practice difficult behavior: We become part of the problem.

2. *Slippery imprecision*. Most books have no rigorous standards from which these categories or labels are derived. Often "straw-people" stereotypes and caricatures are derived anecdotally from experience but are untested. While it may be tempting or amusing to label others, it is seldom helpful. Such labels are merely sophisticated put-downs: schoolyard immaturity translated into churchly vocabulary.

3. *Lack of qualification for diagnoses*. Oates and Bagby are helpful in their careful delineation of problem behaviors. But here too caution is needed. While their treatments give insight into others (and also, they emphasize, insight into ourselves), few of us are equipped to diagnose the categories they name. While we may have some familiarity with *DSM-III* or *DSM-IV*, most of us are not qualified to use and apply it to others.

4. *Labeling is destructive*: Edwin Friedman goes so far as to say that labeling can destroy a person and a relationship with that person, increase

the labeled person's dependency, and "fix" perceptions of how labeled people are seen.[2]

5. *Labeling can be a self-fulfilling prophecy.* As we saw in the story about the school, labeling makes it difficult for new behavior or functions to emerge. We assume that others cannot act otherwise. Furthermore, people often live up to the role assigned to them by their context: If labeled "difficult" or "troublemaker," they may not deign to act otherwise, or we may fail to recognize the change when they do behave differently. Labels can be self-fulfilling.

6. *Labeling is judgmental.* Labeling is a paternalistic and authoritarian approach that pretends to be "objective rather than judgmental."[3] The gospels are full of sayings and stories in which Jesus warns against being judgmental. "Do not judge, so that you may not be judged" (Matt. 7:1).

7. *Labeling reveals our own anxiety.* When we diagnose people rather than relationships, we show that our own anxiety has increased. Labeling is itself a warning sign of something unhealthy in the system.

8. *Labeling makes it easy to write off others' concerns.* Labeling others is too enticing. Whenever someone disagrees with us or challenges us, we can be tempted to regard that person as a "dragon" or a "clergy-killer"! Rather than engage real issues and concerns, attend to legitimate needs, and listen to healthy differences, the temptation is to write off the other party's issues, needs, or concerns. Leadership involves learning from, taking seriously, assimilating, benefiting from, and growing in the face of criticism, adversity, and even adversaries.

9. *Labeling hurts healthy process.* Labeling does not help the process but makes it worse. Not only does diagnosis reveal anxiety; it intensifies it. Most of us will not move toward calmness if we believe a "clergy-killer's" crosshairs are focused on us!

10. *Labeling can be a disguise for projection.* In projection we attribute to others (project onto them) parts of ourselves that we do not want to acknowledge. We shall deal in more depth with projection later. Often projection involves our negative side ("shadow side," poor motives, or despised emotions). Jesus warned against projection:

> "Why do you see the speck in your neighbor's eye, but do not notice the log in your own eye? Or how can you say to your neighbor, 'Let me take the speck out of your eye,' while the log is in your own eye? You hypocrite, first take the log out of your own eye" (Matt. 7:4-5).

11. *Labeling is pastorally irresponsible.* When one labels another pejoratively, one is tempted not to take that person seriously, listen, pay attention, or have compassion. That attitude is a serious failure of a pastor's covenant and ethical obligations.

Several pastors and I met with the late Henri Nouwen, Dutch priest and writer, for a private retreat in which he gave us advice on pastoring. During a day of many memories and intense conversation, one noteworthy moment came when he advised us on creating community.

> One of the essential qualities of creating community . . . is not to judge. Essential. Do not even in your heart figure out, "He's just a jerk." Try to get beyond that. As soon as you start dividing your parishioners into jerks and non-jerks, you're lost, because community is primarily an interior thing. Everybody has to have a space inside you. . . . That doesn't mean you have to be stupid and let everybody walk over you. There should be compassion. People have to know that in your heart that there is space for them.

Nouwen's advice has the sensibility of the Sermon on the Mount. He reminded me of Jesus' warning: "If you insult a brother or sister, you will be liable to the council; and if you say, 'You fool,' you will be liable to the hell of fire" (Matt. 5:22). Insulting or labeling others is contrary to the spirit of Christ.

As pastors, we fail whenever we divide parishioners into "jerks" and "non-jerks." The first rule, then, for dealing with difficult behavior in the congregation is this: Never call a parishioner a "jerk"! Therefore we must focus not on "difficult people" but on "difficult relationships" and "difficult behavior"—a subtle but crucial distinction.

Since neither general self-help approaches nor church-focused reflections have proved helpful, we need to look to a broader understanding for help with these challenging issues. We find this in family-systems thinking, which teaches us to beware of labeling, diagnosing, or blaming "identified patients" or scapegoats. Diagnosing and labeling overlook other causes and variables. Family-systems thinking discourages the simplistic linear thinking of cause-and-effect or labeling's overfocus on singular causation. We will take a closer look at systems thinking later.

Nouwen's advice also reminds us that as we engage these important topics, the issues and stakes go far beyond finding smooth ways to resolve conflict or to facilitate group dynamics. These are serious spiritual issues and struggles. While we are tempted to label others as having spiritual problems, the real challenge is to recognize the opportunity for spiritual growth that *we* have in the face of difficult behavior.

The Case of the Mistaken Teacher

Labeling, treating, or regarding people as "difficult" can mislead us in many ways.

The Quaker scholar Parker Palmer is regarded as a preeminent educator in North America whose books and workshops are deservedly popular. In *The Courage to Teach* he tells a revealing story about his unhelpful dealings with a "difficult" student.[4] Palmer conducts many training sessions for faculty. After teaching for 25 years, he visited a university campus where he was given the opportunity to teach a political-science class for an hour. Of two-and-a-half-dozen students there, Palmer noticed only the "Student from Hell." He became obsessed with this student, who slouched at the back of the room, had neither pen nor paper, kept his cap pulled over his eyes, and wore a coat as if he meant to escape at the first possible opportunity. Palmer says: "I committed the most basic mistake of the greenest neophyte: I became totally obsessed with him, and everyone else in the room disappeared from my screen."

Palmer directed all his attention toward the young man, hoping to awaken or to stir some interest or response. But nothing resulted. "I left that class with a powerful combination of feelings: self-pity, fraudulence, and rage." Moreover, he blamed the "Student from Hell."

Later, he looked forward to his flight home. When the college van picked him up, he was distressed to see that the driver was—you guessed it!—the "Student from Hell." Palmer was unhappy at the prospect of spending time with this young man. The driver asked him whether they might talk. Palmer was reluctant but of course agreed. They had a long conversation and after that corresponded for a time.

The gist of the conversation was that the young man was having great difficulty completing college. His unemployed, alcoholic father made life hard for the youth and actively campaigned to discourage him from studies. The youth looked to Palmer for help and motivation. Palmer saw clearly how this student—like so many students and, we might add, like so many parishioners—was full of fear. "The Student from Hell is not born that way but is created by conditions beyond his or her control," says Palmer.

And that mind-set of openness is also required of church leaders if we are ever tempted to consider parishioners "Jerks from Hell."

CHAPTER 2

Mending a "Body of Broken Bones"

An unhappy faction in a conflicted church communicated its dissent every Sunday morning. Instead of putting money in the offering plates, parishioners deposited notes that said simply, "Resign." The donations took a serious downturn, and the pastor did eventually step down.

Although many resources on difficult behavior leave much to be desired, that does not mean that there are no helpful perspectives. I grieve for the pastors forced out by the empty offering plates. I long for church leaders to find better ways of dealing with conflict.

While we should not label, we must take a deliberate look at the serious problem of difficult behavior in the church.

Are Churches Vulnerable to Intense Conflict?

We need to look at a commonly held assumption: Are churches particularly vulnerable to intense conflict and difficult behavior?

Not surprisingly, books focused on such behavior in congregations insist that congregations are susceptible. Kenneth Haugk, pastor and clinical psychologist, asserts that "antagonists" often have more power in churches than in other places:

> For too long, congregations have been places where antagonists can operate with success. Their behavior is not as successful in many other areas of life because in those areas it is simply not tolerated.[1]

We read such remarks with caution, however, as antagonist-focused books often come from a perspective of anxious overreaction and labeling.

More careful writers, however, make similar observations. Kenneth Alan Moe, a Presbyterian pastor to pastors, worries about the implicit or actual power of some.

> Mentally unhealthy or maladjusted people may be few in number . . . but they tend to wield influence well beyond their numbers. Only one or two disturbed people on a church board may undermine the mission of the congregation and render ineffective the leadership of the pastor. . . . I have seen churches protect and support the mentally sickest . . . , all in the name of love and charity.[2]

This pastor to pastors has serious concerns and is not alone. Anthony Pappas, an expert on small churches, notes that in warm and tolerant congregations, "People with power needs or other pathologies find . . . a viable environment to act out their internal illness."[3]

Even those working from a family-systems paradigm observe the church's particular vulnerability to difficult behavior. In a section called "The Tyranny of the Weak," theology professors Paul Stevens and Phil Collins claim: "Many emotionally and spiritually weak people . . . dominate the church. They often appear emotionally fragile, and people around them 'walk on eggshells.'"[4] Stevens and Collins contend that such folk have extraordinary power: "The seemingly weak member of a family or a church is the most powerful, organizing everyone around his or her needs."

Church consultant Peter L. Steinke bleakly answers the question of whether churches are more prone and vulnerable to difficult behavior by quoting Edwin Friedman:

> Actually religious institutions are the worst offenders at encouraging immaturity and irresponsibility. In church after church, some member is passively-aggressively holding the whole system hostage, and no one wants to fire him or force her to leave because it wouldn't be "the Christian thing to do."[5]

If churches are vulnerable to devastating conflict and difficult behavior, our next challenge is to understand why.

Why Are Churches Vulnerable?

Numerous factors contribute to this vulnerability to difficult behavior and devastating conflict.

1. *"Accomplices" of difficult behavior*. It is tempting to blame "antagonists" or their "difficult behavior," but the responsibility must be spread further. People often permit, if not encourage or enable, immature behavior. This enabling can be done to avoid the hard work of confronting and working out problems or just "to be nice," which Steinke considers "sloppy agape."[6] We often do not know how to be civil and polite and to confront at the same time.

Pastors are often accomplices in helping to perpetuate difficult behavior. They may do so out of a need to please and to be liked—clear instances of codependence.

2. *Passive Responses*. To placate or appease an antagonist can encourage the difficult behavior. Attacks, brinkmanship, ultimatums, authoritarianism, and threats to withhold or withdraw participation, attendance, and finances—all can be effective when the congregation's or leader's highest value is peace or harmony at all costs.

In my nonresistant, pacifist Mennonite tradition, this passivity is complicated by our reading of Jesus' Sermon on the Mount (a text particularly beloved and esteemed by Anabaptists), when he urged us not to resist evil or evildoers (Matt. 5:39). Along with that passage, Jesus' command to forgive "seventy times seven" (Matt. 18:21) lends itself to an easy interpretation of acquiescence to difficult behavior. I suspect, however, that Mennonites are not the only Christians with such problems.

Sometimes, out of naïveté, church people fail to confront inappropriate behavior. We find it difficult to believe that fellow members could do harmful things, perhaps even do them deliberately. Thus it has been hard for churches to deal with and respond to sexual abuse. We want to believe that people always misbehave from the best intentions.

3. *Rituals and social constraints*. Management consultant Robert Bramson notes that certain people learn to use "rituals and social constraints . . . to create a protected place."[7]

Telemarketers, for example, take advantage of "rituals and social constraints." Making intrusive phone calls at inconvenient times and failing to ask permission to continue speaking must work to some degree, or telemarketers would not persist. My family has often compared notes with others about how difficult it is to deal politely with such calls, assuming that one can get in a word edgewise! We have learned to say simply and calmly: "I'm sorry; we do not do uninvited business or accept charitable solicitations over the phone." Telemarketers now generally accept my explanation politely. Even so, I do not feel comfortable when the occasional telemarketer responds rudely, sounds hurt, or (as occasionally happens) accuses me of hard-heartedness.

As I write, I look out the window and see an example closer to home for people of faith: a religious group that also exploits "rituals and social constraints." I have been in countless conversations with sincere, well-meaning, hospitable, gentle, believing, tolerant, churchgoing Christians who do not know how to deal with door-to-door evangelists. Christians often have a hard time setting boundaries. Many choose not to answer the door. Some mild-mannered people are curt almost to the point of rudeness if they do answer the door. This behavior reminds us how hard it is to set boundaries in the face of people who are persistent, intrusive, and aggressive; who will not take "no" for an answer; and who will not listen to another's point of view. We have the same boundary-setting difficulties in our churches.

4. *A further bind: the price of togetherness.* "Rituals and social constraints" are more pronounced in congregations of people who choose to be together. Many are willing to pay a high price to remain together. Some churches value togetherness and fellowship above almost anything else. In such places, it can be considered bad form to raise any challenges . . . even to those whose behavior is challenging! Rather than "make waves," members tolerate difficult behavior and so allow its perpetuation.

5. *The interior stakes.* Church-conflict expert Hugh Halverstadt notes other reasons why church fights are so devastating. For one, he argues, the interior stakes are high:

> Spiritual commitments and faith understandings are highly inflammable because they are central to one's psychological identity. When Christians differ over beliefs or commitments, they may question or even condemn one another's spirituality or character. Their self-esteem is on the line. That is why parties slip so easily into taking differences personally, even launching personal attacks. When church folk feel that their worldview or personal integrity is being questioned or condemned, they often become

emotionally violent and violating. Any means are used to justify their goal of emotional self-protection.[8]

6. *The eternal stakes of church conflict.* Because of theological beliefs, people are often convinced that salvation itself is at stake: their own, their children's, or the church's. Once people hold the conviction that the eternal consequences of a dispute mean salvation or damnation, then there may be no holds barred (even in supposedly nonresistant, pacifist faith traditions). This situation is especially complicated when we are not aware of our personal agenda or when church fights are not acknowledged to grow out of personal agendas.

The church I serve is a historic congregation almost two centuries old. Major theological rifts were fought there over the years, including the 19th-century battles that led to the splitting off of groups that eventually became Old Order Mennonites and also to "New Mennonites" (as the present Missionary Church was first called).

Ironically, despite our allegedly gentle and nonresistant tradition, averse to state intervention and lawsuits, we are now in possession of our building only because of a major 19th-century power play: A small cadre of the "old guard" used a deed to wrest control of the building from new-thinking revivalists.

In a more recent church conflict, protagonists declared that our denomination was going to hell, and they felt it necessary to save our small congregation from that fate. The motive sounded worthy, but the fight and the zealotry that ensued were undignified, abrasive, and ugly. Such examples illustrate the reason for a frequent family rule in our society: Be careful about discussing religion. Many families avoid the subject of religion altogether: Such discussions are too intense, painful, and apparently irresolvable. The woman who cuts my hair tells me that the only training she ever received in dealing with people is one piece of advice: Do not discuss religion or politics; they are too inflammatory and controversial.

7. *Religious language can preclude healthy discernment.* Unfortunately, religious language and rhetoric do not always lead to self-awareness. Like the title characters of the film *The Blues Brothers*, some people think that being "on a mission from God" justifies all kinds of absurd behavior. I have known several church officers, for example, who insisted that they were called by God to the post for life. This conviction did not make it easier to discuss a transition of office or to consider a more careful discernment of gifts.

8. *The pressures of high goals.* The church is a place for our highest goals, values, priorities, and expectations. We often bring expectations that are higher than those we have for any other relationships. And when we are let down by our other relationships—family, work, society—the pressure is even greater for the church to meet our unmet needs.

Yet no institution can meet all our expectations. Often expectations are not *spoken*, even if they are recognized (which is by no means assured). The disillusion and anger that result from the clash of expectations and ensuing disappointments all too often lead to anger, intense conflict, and even abuse.

9. *Challenging the status quo.* The Gospel calls for social and personal transformation. Many stories in the gospels and Acts show how Jesus and his followers challenged and upset religious and political leaders and a whole host of social mores. Challenging the status quo generates emotional heat.[9] It is then not surprising that Jesus and many of his followers lost their lives. The Gospel still raises unsettling questions and challenges many givens and assumptions. Going up against the status quo is a risky business, one that makes us susceptible to difficult behavior and reactivity.

One sees the dangers by remembering the tremendous energy and friction in churches throughout North America and elsewhere in recent decades over such issues as civil rights and integration, the ordination of women, and the status of homosexuals.

10. *Volunteer organizations and inappropriate uses of power*: The church's voluntary nature also exacerbates difficult behavior and the intensity of church conflicts. The fact that people volunteer may make others unable to recognize inappropriate behavior or to hold people to account. Members refuse to recognize destructive behavior in those who attend regularly, give sacrificially, or volunteer extensively. Members recognize only reluctantly the shadow side of such folk and fear losing their attendance, gifts, or volunteer efforts.

Sometimes people who hold no office wield power nonetheless. A church-council chair once complained of the influence of some in the congregation who "can get their way without coming to any meetings or even saying a word in public."

Voluntary organizations sometimes lend themselves to concentrations or abuse of power. A church board was composed of four members—two of whom were husband and wife. The couple were the treasurer and the chair, holding the two most powerful positions and co-signing all checks. All meetings were conducted in their home. They ran the church nomination process and were always re-elected by acclamation. (Such inappropriately concentrated power, by the way, contravenes Canadian government guidelines for charitable institutions.)

11. *The effect of excluding some from power*: The flip side: While some have too much power, others may have too little. Often misbehavior has to do with how *little* power people have. It is not only those wielding power who act out. People may act out to get attention if they feel neglected, to accomplish something when they feel powerless, or to express the anger of their frustrations.

When I began one pastorate, I visited many new parishioners at home. In separate visits, two families told me that they were "only newcomers" to the church. My caution signals were alerted because both families had been attending for more than 25 years. Both were frustrated about not being part of the church's leadership and not having their points of view represented in congregational decisions. Not surprisingly, within two years of my arrival both families acted disruptively and destructively, with one family ultimately leaving in anger.

12. *The hazards of small organizations*: Some believe that the relative smallness of many congregations (or even the *ideal* of smallness) makes them more susceptible to difficult behavior. A colleague says that small churches are like little puddles: each wave of conflict, upset, or controversy washes over and affects everyone, muddying issues, and leaving all feeling sullied. Perhaps so, but I have also seen large congregations preoccupied for years with the antics of small groups.

The *vulnerability* of being small also contributes here. In small churches, leaders are sometimes unwilling to deal with inappropriate or abusive behavior out of fear that the person in question might withdraw volunteer involvements or financial contributions. Thus small churches may tolerate behavior that other institutions reject.

In one small congregation, a major contributor was given to strong opinions and extreme views. Sometimes one phrase in a sermon would upset her so much that she would absent herself from the church for months, withholding offerings and informing others of her actions. Every year, this woman helped persuade at least one household to leave the church. More than one congregational leader warned: "We must not offend her. We cannot afford to lose her contributions."

13. *Other contributors to difficult behavior*: Specific circumstances can increase the possibility of intense church conflict or difficult behavior. There is, for example, the problem of dealing with the "pastoral ghost"

memories and legacy (good or bad) of a previous long-term or especially influential pastor.

Some conditions can intensify troubled behavior: the loss of a long-tenured pastor, a series of short-term pastorates, a traumatic incident in the church, poorly defined structures or policies, building programs, sexual boundary-crossing by clergy, a membership decrease or increase, tensions within the denomination, and a restructure or reorganization.[10]

Nevertheless, Edwin Friedman says that such changes do not automatically cause problems or difficulties. If conflict or difficult behavior does occur, it usually functions in combination with other circumstances:

> No issue merely by the nature of its content is automatically more
> virulent than another. Congregations can be rent asunder or fire
> their ministers over the same issue that, under other homeostatic
> conditions, will go quietly away.[11]

The impact of the issue always depends on other conditions in the system.

Social change can also contribute to an increase in difficult, irrational behavior. Our era faces great and rapid change, and this factor affects all relational systems. Thus now more than ever, it is in our interest to understand difficult behavior in congregations.

Cautions About Focusing on Difficult Behavior

In exploring the reasons for a proclivity of many churches to "host" destructive conflict and unhealthy difficult behavior, it is still too easy and tempting to blame others for problems in our churches. Therefore, several important cautions are in order.

1. *Self-understanding.* Leaders should make a primary priority of understanding our own difficult behavior rather than being preoccupied with that of others. "Why do you see the speck in your neighbor's eye, but do not notice the log in your own eye?" (Matt. 7:3). Leaders also exhibit difficult behavior.

This caution is put most forcefully by pastoral psychologist Conrad W. Weiser. He worries about the "attraction of less-than-fully functioning persons to religious professions" who are "at risk for future difficulty," especially because "religious professionals are often less amenable to change." He warns: "Religious systems attract dysfunctional persons."[12]

2. *Respecting others*: It is easy to write off as "difficult" the behavior that we dislike or behavior that is eccentric or inconvenient, unappealing or unattractive. Like it or not, protagonists, adversaries, conflict, tension, eccentric, irrational, and immature behavior, and even a "loyal opposition" are a natural and healthy given in churches.

Perhaps one reason churches do not always respond to "difficult behavior" as clergy might prefer is that the members understand some realities that the clergy do not. Churches, like families, are often willing and able to put up with behavior that seems nonsensical to an outsider. A pastor is almost always an outsider to the system and may misread the seriousness of a situation; i.e., overreact.

I learned this truth during my first pastorate in the inner city of Chicago. There was much about certain members' behavior that I found perplexing (or worse). One of my seminary professors, Carl Dudley, helped me appreciate the roles and behaviors that seemed to me quaint and perplexing at the best of times and difficult and outrageous at other times. Learning from Dudley, we might even come to enjoy, appreciate, be amused by, or celebrate the antics of eccentrics who once struck us as merely difficult. We might even find the freedom to be characters ourselves! When we expect and anticipate eccentric behavior, our appreciation can increase and we are more prepared to receive and enjoy it as a gift.

At my first annual church meeting as a pastor, the treasurer and a prominent member (and large contributor) quickly launched into a heated discussion about finances. I was alarmed and felt my pulse accelerate, wondering what would happen next and whether I needed to act. Then another church member guffawed about the brother and sister "going at it again." Sure enough, only then did I remember that the treasurer and the prominent member were siblings; this spat was a playful routine that they re-enacted regularly. The heat generated was not a serious concern. The members and even the antagonists had a hearty laugh, and everyone moved on with the business at hand. Parishioner "insiders" understood something that the "outsider" pastor did not.

3. *Beware of exclusion.* Emphasis on difficult behavior can tempt us to exclude those whose behavior does not fit our standards. Churches should expect to include and embrace misfits. "Those who are well have no need of a physician, but those who are sick; I have come to call not the righteous but sinners" (Mark 2:17). The old adage is true that churches are more hospitals for sinners than museums for saints.

Every church I have served as pastor had its characters and misfits

who were social outcasts—unemployable, delusional, dysfunctional, or dis-
reputable. Their behavior was not always congenial, and sometimes it was
difficult. Yet the congregation and I were (usually) grateful for their presence and (often) glad that the church provided at least one place where
they could consistently experience God's love. Sometimes the church seems
to have more than its per-capita share of difficult people: If so, we just
might be doing our job. (Welcoming and including such folk, however, is
not the same as allowing their agenda to determine or direct the church's
agenda.)

4. *Reality of brokenness*. Difficult behavior and destructive conflict
are not merely a matter of right-versus-wrong or the creation of a healthy
church. The problem of difficult behavior is a tragic inevitability that we
must learn to face and live with as broken, sinful, wounded people striving
to learn how to live, work, worship, fellowship, and engage in mission
together. As Trappist monk and author Thomas Merton writes in a vividly
compelling image:

> As long as we are on earth, the love that unites us will bring us
> suffering by our very contact with one another, because this love
> is the resetting of a Body of broken bones. Even saints cannot
> live with saints on this earth without some anguish, without some
> pain at the differences that come between them.
>
> There are two things [people] can do about the pain of dis-
> union with other [people]. They can love or they can hate. [13]

Introducing Family Systems

If most books that address difficult behavior begin by labeling people who
trouble us, we need to approach our concerns with a "bigger picture,"
trying to understand the broader context. Such an approach is offered in
applying family-systems theory.

As we review major ideas of systems thinking, we will immediately
see many implications for understanding ways of responding to conflict
and difficult behavior.

1. *Emotional units*: The first principle of systems thinking is to view
groups, families, institutions, or churches as emotional units: A system is
always more than the sum of its parts. The human body is more than a

collection of individual parts; thus Paul's metaphor of the church as body fits well with systems thinking. "For as in one body we have many members, and not all the members have the same function, so we, who are many, are one body in Christ, and individually we are members of one another" (Rom. 12:4-6).

Individual behavior must be examined, but as it relates to the relational system as a whole. For example, while a parishioner's difficult behavior may involve individual responsibility and choice, nevertheless his or her actions are part of a larger whole. Those who work with addictions, for example, know that addictions and abuse are often enabled by codependent family members.

It is never enough to examine an individual's actions in isolation. Even people who behave poorly (e.g., proverbial "black sheep") may act out the needs of a group: Often if that poorly behaved individual left, someone else would take his or her place.

A member was unhappy with the theology of his pastor and board. He had many heated discussions with selected members about theological issues—discussions that they found mutually frustrating. A climate of tension prevailed in the church. These discussions appeared to be initiated by the individual alone. Finally, the unhappy parishioner left for a more theologically compatible church. Leaders heaved a sigh of relief, assuming that the controversy was finished. But another person took up the mantle of articulating dissent. This pattern was repeated several times: a dissenter apparently stirred up heated discussions, then left in disappointment, and soon another dissenter arose in his or her place. For some reason the dissenters were unconsciously designated by the group to ventilate concerns.

The role played by the group does not deny the importance of individual responsibility. Systems thinking does not quickly reduce analyses to either/or, black-or-white. It is not simply a matter of either individual responsibility or systems causation. Systems theory does not look for people to blame but sees responsibility throughout the system. That point leads to our second observation about family systems.

2. *Multiple causation.* Systems theorists look for multiple causation when problems arise. No single issue or challenge suffices to cause problems. Causation is not straight and linear but mutually influenced. Thus in examining any conflict or so-called difficult behavior, we look for a number of contributing factors, not merely for a presenting issue or a villain, whether a scapegoat or "identified patient."

3. *Interdependence*. Members of a system are interdependent and interrelated. This too is exemplified by Paul's body imagery: "The eye cannot say to the hand, 'I have no need of you,' nor again the head to the feet, 'I have no need of you'" (1 Cor. 12:21). Something that affects one element of a system also affects others. Systems are like a suspended mobile: when one part is touched, moved, or shifted, each of the other parts is set in motion. The interrelatedness of parts can create "synergy": The interaction of the whole produces more energy than simply adding up the possibilities of the individuals themselves. This interrelatedness can also make it very difficult to sort out what is actually happening!

Members of a system have two paradoxical needs that affect all their relations and exist in continual tension: the need to be separate (differentiation) versus the need to be close (fusion)—also called the need to be "me" versus the need to be "we."[14]

In studying difficult behavior, we must examine how this tension between differentiation and fusion plays a role. Ironically, what looks like differentiation may actually be fusion. Sometimes people get close to leaders by picking fights and thus getting the attention they desire!

4. *Relationship to family of origin*. People's behavior in a congregation (or any social group) often parallels behavior in their family of origin. At the very least, it is crucial for pastors to understand their own family-of-origin issues. Also, when dealing with "difficult" or "troublesome" people, it is helpful to understand *their* family relationships. Self-differentiation is related to family of origin: If members are not differentiated at home, they are not likely to be differentiated in church. Realizing this, the pastor might deal a little less anxiously with behavior that appears "difficult" or "troublesome." When possible, this connection would mean that a church could try to work with a whole family, not just an individual.

Thus for the best possible systems interpretation of conflict or difficult behavior it is helpful to know about and understand members' family histories and relationships.

5. *Stability and change*. All systems need a tension of stability and change. Yet systems mostly resist change. Thus actions often provoke reactions and backlashes. Such backlashes are called "homeostasis" or "change back!" reactions.[15] Changes in a system lead to anxiety and may provoke reactions to restore the prior status quo.

A couple raised their family in a congregation. Over the years, all but one child either moved to another church or stopped attending altogether.

Then the last child also left, taking her spouse and children. Within weeks, the nonattending son (whose name was the same as the departing son-in-law's!) returned to church with his children and became actively involved. Here both the family system and the congregational family system appeared to collaborate to ensure that this couple still had children and grandchildren in the church.

6. *Multigenerational patterns and problems.* This phenomenon is further complicated by the fact that many problems are multigenerational, passed down from "generation to generation," as the title of Friedman's book reminds us. No matter what changes in the group, then, similar problems may re-emerge and recur.

In dealing with difficult behavior, one takes into consideration the history of a particular church. Are there larger patterns of recurring conflict that may play a role? A church I served had a pattern of experiencing a major conflict every ten years and then settling down to a decade of relative calm. Some churches have a pattern of "upsetting the basket" and replacing their pastors with disturbing regularity.

7. *Triangulation.* When two people become anxious or uncomfortable with each other, one or both may "triangle" a third party into the relationship. When intensity becomes too high between people, a third element is made part of the picture. Some married people "triangle" by having a child or overfocusing on the child, consulting too closely with one's in-laws, or having an affair with another man or woman—or with one's job! Some adolescents or young adults deal with family tensions by marrying or cohabiting.

Individuals can triangle churches. It is not unusual for someone in conflict at home with a spouse, child, parent, or sibling to "pick fights" at church as a way of getting his or her attention off the truly painful family. Or a person might complain about the family member at church, choosing to be seen as a victim.

This triangling can work in other ways too. People may become overinvolved in volunteering and "doing the good work" of the church as a way of ignoring or avoiding needed work at home. We generally appreciate hardworking volunteers, but we need to recognize that even volunteering for good causes can have a shadow side!

Triangling also occurs when a person intervenes and tries to change the relationship between others. Marital or family therapy is complicated because it often involves the tricky aspect of dealing with triangles. Thus it is generally advisable for pastors *not* to practice ongoing marital or family therapy: It is almost impossible to be a pastor to all parties, especially when relationships are highly conflicted.

Gossip is a form of triangling. Alas, "grapevines" often thrive in churches. We may take it as a compliment to be told secrets about someone else, but that is triangling. Pastors are prime candidates for triangling. (How often does a family member or one-half of a married couple complain to a pastor about another family member as a way of getting the pastor to see his or her side!) Yet we are called to serve as pastor to all in our congregation; we must be careful about taking sides in conflicts or triangles.

Triangles are a way to deal with anxiety and "bind" it so that actual issues are not addressed. One nuclear family can have a host of dysfunctional triangles. In a healthy triangle, roles are not fixed and rigid but flexible. In an unhealthy triangle, roles are unchangeable and patterns are repeated over and again.

Understanding triangles, we see that we can work only on ourselves and our own relationships. We cannot directly change other people or relationships. The challenge in triangles is to be a "nonanxious presence," a concept we shall consider later.

One challenge in dealing with conflict and difficult behavior is helping people to communicate directly rather than forming unhealthy triangles or grapevines to deal with (but actually increase) their anxiety. We shall return to this topic later. Pastors need to be wary of triangles, to identify them to others, and to avoid initiating triangles.

Later, as we also consider the responsibilities of pastors in the face of difficult behavior, we shall see that the way we deal with triangles is crucial.

Implications of Family Systems

Let us unpack insights that family-systems thinking gives into what drives difficult behavior.

Family-systems theory cautions against being too quick to name, blame, or label people who might be seen as troublemakers, "black sheep," "identified patients," or scapegoats. If someone's behavior seems inappropriate, we explore whether the family system's dis-ease is emerging there.

A family-systems approach is not naïve about difficult behavior, but it does caution us as to how we understand that behavior. While it can be troubling and serious, difficult behavior is not the main or central problem. It is a symptom of more serious problems, dis-ease, anxiety, or ill health in the system. In medicine, we do not bring healing merely by treating symptoms. Similarly, in churches we look beyond symptoms. Church-conflict experts Charles Cosgrove and Dennis Hatfield doubt that individuals who exhibit difficult behavior can be directly changed because "individuals don't change unless change happens in the systems in which they live." They question several common approaches to difficult behavior: counseling and referrals to therapy, political maneuverings, and even conflict mediation. These methods often fail. Counseling and therapy often overlook systems dynamics. Political power plays serve to mask or evict symptoms and often increase anxiety and ill health. Conflict management is limited when "people don't always reveal their real complaints. Often they prefer to mask what's really bothering them by fighting over other issues."[16]

Difficult behavior is often a sign that something else is amiss. The behavior is not the problem but indicates that something deeper has gone wrong. Yet another function of difficult behavior may be to keep people preoccupied and distracted from real issues. Some churches spend so much time and energy (in meetings and elsewhere) reacting to difficult behavior that they never deal with the real internal issues that face the body as a whole.

Family-systems theory shows that systems may implicitly allow, use, and even encourage troublemaking. Someone regarded by most as a troublemaker may be not only tolerated but perhaps also encouraged. For example, a difficult person might usefully keep another potential power person (board member or pastor, for example) in line or prevent the leader from acquiring too much power. In a congregation anxious that membership growth is too rapid and unsettling, a "difficult person" can help deter too many new people from staying. Keeping out unwelcome newcomers may be a nasty job, but someone has to do it!

Difficult-behavior symptoms may not in fact be directly resolvable or even manageable. Therefore family-systems thinking generally recommends working with a system as a whole rather than trying to change dysfunctional parts. Systems thinking encourages us to look at those symptoms as signs of something important that is happening below the surface, and to respond to those dynamics and phenomena instead.

Now we turn to look at some of those "below the surface" phenomena.

CHAPTER 3

Hazards, Hazards Everywhere

Glancing over the minutes of a church committee, the pastor noted that several decisions had been made at a meeting; yet she knew that most committee members were not present on the date cited in the minutes. When she checked with the chair, he responded: "Four persons were at the meeting: the Father, the Son, the Spirit, and me. We made the decisions that I recorded in those minutes." What would you do if faced with such a situation?

With our family-systems understandings, we are now in a good position to look at some of the deeper dynamics that create particular hazards for difficult behavior.

Transference and Countertransference

During his first year in our church, a parishioner enthusiastically greeted me every week after the service. He energetically pumped my hand and fervently complimented my "great sermon." One Sunday my sermon was controversial. That day the man averted his gaze and stepped through the sanctuary doors as far from me as possible. After that, he avoided speaking to me. Within months, he tried to organize others to oust me. When unsuccessful, he left in anger, saying I was a deceitful heretic.

Have you ever been attacked for no apparent reason and thought, "I didn't deserve that"? Have you ever witnessed an inexplicable outburst and wondered, "What was that all about?" Most pastors have had such experiences. Transference and projection contribute to behavior that is bewildering, confusing, and occasionally appalling.

Leaders are often the uncomfortable focus of difficult behavior and interrelational distortions. We might be the target of intense and aggressive conflict or difficult behavior. Although we may not anticipate (let alone appreciate) such treatment, we need to expect and understand it.

The intensity of church conflicts, especially those involving or directed at pastors, often has to do with transference or projection (the latter term is discussed in the next section). Transference and projection impede people from seeing and understanding one another clearly. They not only distort reality, but also *evade* reality.

Mansell Pattison, professor of psychiatry, notes that Freud first recognized and studied transference. Freud

> found that in his administration of psychoanalytic treatment the patient sometimes began to treat him *as if* he, the therapist, were some emotionally important figure from the patient's prior life. To Freud it seemed that the patient, loaded with disturbing ideas and feelings out of the past, simply "transferred" them onto the figure of the psychoanalyst. Almost like an electrical short circuit, the transfer took place as it were "through a false connection." Feeling memories out of the past were applied directly to the current situation. The reoccurrence of childhood developmental conflicts and their transference in therapy to other persons and relationships reflected a renewed attempt to resolve those conflicts with a new figure.[1]

Transference is an interpersonal distortion: people relate to another *now* on the basis of *past* significant relationships, ignoring or distorting present realities. This reaction happens in both counseling and pastoral care, but it can be more readily attended to in counseling. In counseling it can be named and used in the therapy. Transference is much more difficult to address in daily life or in pastoral care, where the reaction is often assumed to be accurate. Transference relationships often move quickly and unconsciously toward extremes of affection or hostility.

While transference is a relational distortion, two things must be recognized.[2] First, it is normal, and virtually everyone experiences it. Do not disdain those who exhibit transference, or be surprised or annoyed by it. Second, transference can be essential to healing and at its best is a temporary distortion. There is a potential blessing in transference: People are given a safer opportunity to address previously unresolved issues. Transference is not always dramatic; it does not always involve a "blowup" or "acting out."

Our role as pastors thrusts us into the emotional intensity of transference. We are prime candidates for such distortions. People may react to pastors with all the confusion, ambivalence, hostility, or distortion that they bring to relationships with or memories of their parents or God. In some faith traditions, priests are even addressed as "Father." More than that, clergy may be associated with many unresolved family issues. Considering how loosely family language is bandied about in churches, it is no wonder that congregations are hotbeds of transference. Pastors, by virtue of position and role, almost automatically become part of the mixed-up morass of ideas and feelings (positive or negative) that people have about God or their parents.

Transference can also occur in connection with *previous pastors*.

A member may view the pastor as good and kind, even though in reality the pastor may be brusque and uncaring, because the parishioner transfers to the pastor the previously experienced attributes of another pastor known in childhood.

Many pastors today enjoy free rides courtesy of the behavior of pastors several generations ago. Problems occur, however, when a parishioner has had a traumatic relationship with a pastor in childhood or at some other vulnerable time. The current pastor may be feared or mistrusted for the sins of another pastor.[3]

Difficult experiences with previous pastors, inadequate or conflicted terminations, and positive feelings toward previous much-beloved pastors all can create problems of "pastoral ghosts," seeing present pastors through the prism of their predecessors.

The stakes are high. Transference and countertransference (the latter will be examined shortly) are often part of sexual boundary-crossing. The emotional intensity of a pastoral-care or counseling relationship can spark in vulnerable parishioners feelings of amorousness or adoration and render them susceptible to boundary-crossing or initiatives from the pastor that are inappropriate and even harmful. (A similar dynamic is at play when doctors have affairs with patients, teachers or professors with students, and therapists with clients.) It is the responsibility of the professional to see that boundaries are not violated.

The stakes are high in other ways too. Transference and countertransference are not only an individualistic matter between pastor and parishioner. They are often connected to serious congregational conflict. When transference is involved, conflict can get ugly as people's attitudes and motivations are distorted and unconscious.

Since the stakes are high, it is important for leaders to pay attention to such phenomena and to deal with them appropriately. Pastors do not just attract transference; we are particularly vulnerable to it. The parish setting is even more likely than therapy to prompt transference. How can we recognize it?

Pattison says transference may be occurring when a person asks often for attention, reacts differently from others or overreacts, is excessively positive or negative about routine pastoral care, desires counseling in unusual locations or times, requires the pastor to resolve the parishioner's problems or make his or her decisions, fails to keep appointments or fulfill commitments, is overscrupulous in duties.[4] We sometimes recognize transference when we feel confused: Reactions seem misplaced or distorted, or we do not know how to deal with demands. We may feel tempted to do things or act roles that do not feel "true" to us.

Pastors are not only obliged to come to grips with transference. The other side of this equation is our own *countertransference*: the response of a person "in authority" to others' transference. Pattison says it occurs "when one attempts to solve one's own problems through the problems of the parishioner, or vicariously enjoys behavior in the parishioner which one feels one must deny in oneself."[5] Countertransference dynamics closely parallel transference dynamics. Self-awareness is essential to the pastor's operating well and with integrity. Thus understanding our own countertransference is essential.

Pattison proposes a list of countertransference indications: being careless about appointments, repeatedly experiencing erotic or hostile emotions, being bored or inattentive during conversations, permitting or encouraging misbehavior, trying to impress people, arguing frequently, quickly taking sides in conflicts, prematurely reassuring people to lessen the pastor's own anxiety, dreaming repeatedly about a parishioner, believing the parishioner's well-being rests solely with us, behaving differently toward one parishioner than toward others, making appointments at unusual times or places, or behaving in an unusual manner.

Rather than gripe about the transference of others, we must first be aware of our own personality distortions or overreactions. Like parishioners, we often bring previously unresolved relationships into church settings.

While transference and countertransference raise all manner of hazards and difficulties, it is important to be matter-of-fact about them: They are normal. But we should not ignore them, be oblivious to them, or take them for granted. We must be vigilant about them and address them as needed.

Projection

Projection is an interpersonal distortion whose dynamics resemble transference and countertransference. Like them, projection may be the cause of behavior that seems unexpected or overreactive. Again, clergy are good candidates for projection.

In projection, one's own responsibility, problem, interior state, or feelings are attributed elsewhere. A person projects his or her positive or negative feelings, traits, or motives onto another person, group, or thing. This distortion can lead to scapegoating: projecting shadows or negative feelings on someone else. We believe that if we punish or eliminate the other, then *our* problems will be resolved. Extremism and projection are connected. Projection is also closely connected to paranoid personalities: Paranoia can be the projection of extreme anger.[6] When projection becomes paranoid, it is difficult to deal with. Parishioners who project negatively can be a major hazard in ministry.

When we project, we create others, even God, "in our image." People often project their own notions onto their idea of God, a hazard all people of faith must guard against. A Yiddish proverb says that if triangles had a god, it would have three sides!

Projection often involves people in the limelight. The response to Princess Diana's death was a stunning example. In the days following her death, more than a million bouquets were delivered to various landmarks associated with her. At times, all of England appeared (despite its famed "stiff upper lip") to shut down during its unprecedented display of grief. The media accentuated this response by publishing lovely pictures of the fashionable, well-attired, long-limbed, big-eyed Diana. People identified with the princess of Wales, even though her jet-setting life was far distant from daily life in the vast majority of the world. Meanwhile the royal family was the target of another form of projection, the flip side: widespread condemnation for being "coldly" absent while the nation grieved. Projection can attribute either overpositive or overnegative characteristics and feelings to others.

Pastors may be on the receiving end of distorted perceptions, feelings, and opinions. A parishioner may project onto the pastor something from within the parishioner, either unrecognized goodness or unacknowledged hostility.

Once when I was a candidate for a pastorate, a seasoned pastor warned: "Watch out for overly friendly people." Those who appear too eager to know and befriend a pastor may harbor projections. While projections may appear positive at first, they can flip quite easily. Her warning came true: Those who were initially friendly at the candidacy stage became antagonists within a few years.

In a study of forced terminations of Mennonite pastors in Canada, Menno Epp, who himself is a Mennonite pastor, details the *interpersonal incompetence* of those involuntarily terminated. When pastors respond to projection with anger, immobility, hurt, or defensiveness, their reactions often contribute to their dismissal.[7] Once again, we see that the stakes are high.

While pastors are often the "screens" for others' projections, we are capable of projecting negative sides, shadows, or evil onto parishioners or other groups. I know I have! The danger of projection is one reason to be cautious about labeling and categorizing others whose behavior we dislike. Too many resources on dealing with difficult people verge on the projective.

Just as transference and countertransference can quickly and unconsciously slide into either liking or disliking (or even more emotional extremes), so projection is double-edged. It can go to positive or negative extremes (as with the reactions to the death of Princess Diana and the bereavement of the royal family).

While two extremes of projection are possible, most pastors have more problems receiving *negative* projections. We do not care for being perceived as evil, malicious, poorly motivated, or unchristian. But projection, whether negative or positive, always indicates *ambivalence*, even if its appearance is positive. Even idealization can be a cover for hate and anger. Ann Dally, a British psychiatrist, notes that idealization is

a feeling of love towards something or somebody towards whom one actually has feelings of both love and hate. The hate is ignored and so kept from consciousness. The love is unrealistic because it is separated from the hate with which it is actually inextricably connected. Thus it becomes illusory, in that it is supported by distorted or falsified perception which is used unconsciously to prevent the hate from becoming conscious. If it is pointed out that hate is actually present alongside the love, angry reactions are liable to be provoked.[8]

Those who enjoy positive idealization might treat it a little more cautiously if they realize that it is also a cover for negative feelings and even for hate!

Once again, the most important warning about projection must be to and about ourselves. In her memoir *An American Childhood*, essayist Annie Dillard writes: "The interior life is often stupid. Its egoism blinds it and deafens it; its imagination spins out ignorant tales, fascinated."[9] Strange musings these are, from a most inspiring and reflective writer. She recalls a childhood experience of being convinced that a transparent phantom invaded her room and intended to kill her. Terrified, she watched it repeatedly enter her room each night. She dared tell no one, as then the phantom would surely succeed. Finally, she figured out that the phantom was actually the reflections from a passing car's windshield!

This discovery prompted her to stop seeing enemies out there and to look within: "The things in the world did not necessarily cause my overwhelming feelings; the feelings were inside me, beneath my skin, behind my ribs, within my skull. They were even, to some extent, under my control." Dillard's experience is a cautionary tale about overreacting to difficult behavior and perceived antagonism, and monitoring first the most dangerous antagonist of all, the one inside ourselves.

A Humbling Example of Projection

For several years, I visited a monastery monthly for a short retreat. The monks never turned me away, not even when I could not pay. One might reasonably think I would be grateful for their hospitality and fond of the place. But, human creature that I am, my feelings were mixed.

I moved further away and visited only once or twice a year. Over the years the number of monks at this monastery declined. Many of the friendly monks, those who occasionally spoke to me, moved elsewhere. As an introvert, I do not need much chatting, but a friendly word or question during teatime was always welcome, especially on retreats when I was going stir-crazy.

The monks who remained were mostly quiet and reserved. When I encountered one in a hall, he would barely make eye contact. When no one spoke to me during retreats, I interpreted the silence as hostility. I went to the monastery less and less frequently. Finally, I was absent for years.

Then I read that Benedictine monks are duty-bound to give guests space and *not* as a rule to engage them in conversation. Quiet monks, then, are merely being respectful. (Monks also learn "custody of the eyes," the deliberate practice of avoiding eye contact.) Monks who spoke to me may actually have been breaking rules!

I wrote to the monastery, asking for a retreat. The reserved guestmaster wrote a friendly note: "I look forward to seeing you again." I believed him. My sense of being welcome was reinforced upon arrival. The guestmaster did not ask how long I *would* stay, but how long I *could* stay. Later, the abbot gave me a warm "Welcome back," as did other monks. One even waylaid me for a bear hug, telling me how good it was to see me.

I had misread the situation. Almost everything about the monastery was the same: The monks were still reserved. (Some still seemed unfriendly.) But with a new perspective I could see what I had overlooked before. I was impressed that this monastery charges nothing and does not even recommend a minimal contribution (which many monasteries reasonably do). A card in my room read: "We hope you have a pleasant and spiritually fruitful stay. Please visit us again." And I believed this invitation.

The monastery is the same as before. It is I, not the monks, who changed. It was easy for me to project associations on a group of distant men, all wearing the same plain black uniform. (And I probably did my fair share of transference with these men, who are addressed with the emotionally loaded titles "Brother" and "Father.") I am the one who changed when I was more open and receptive, and less judgmental. I was the one who saw things differently; I became more appreciative.

This is also my greatest learning on dealing with difficult behavior in church: Pay attention to yourself first. If you perceive and treat others as enemies, they will look more and more like enemies.

Symbolic Role

We have seen the role of symbolism in transference, with pastors symbolizing God or one's family. It also plays a role in projection, with the other symbolizing one's own inner state. The *symbolism* of the pastoral role itself is also a complicating factor in difficult behavior.

Pattison says parental projections are clearly evident in the case of the three historic professions: law, medicine, and ministry.[10] People attribute to them *omnipresence*: Everyone counts on being able to have a lawyer, a doctor, or a minister. Pastors see evidence of this belief in the reactions that sometimes arise when they are absent from the office during regular hours, are difficult to reach, or happen to be traveling when a crisis arises for a parishioner.

We also, Pattison asserts, attribute *omniscience* to professionals, expecting them to know how to solve any problem or address any crisis. Pastors never know what new crisis or problem might arise. Every time I encountered a "first"—crack addiction, drug overdose, severely deformed newborn, suicide attempt, spousal abuse, family abandonment, terminal diagnosis—parishioners did not ask if I was qualified, request my résumé, or inquire about my academic transcript.

Pattison argues that we also see professionals as *omnipotent*. We trust not only their knowledge but also their ability. Expectations increase as vulnerability grows,

> for during . . . crisis and stress we all tend to regress. That is, we experience ourselves in terms of basic feelings of childhood. We feel threatened, helpless, fearful. Our adult self tends to melt away, and we may feel that old primordial sense out of whose depths we cry: "Mommy, Daddy, where are you—help me." The *thoughts* may not emerge that explicitly, but our feelings and actions reflect the depth of our regressive anguish. At that point, when we seek help from a lawyer, a minister, or a doctor, we are likely to relate to that professional in terms of our childhood need for a succorer Parent-God figure.

When pastors disappoint such expectations, we are vulnerable to a parishioner's extreme acting out or anger.

The minister is not just a *professional* symbol but also a *sacred* one, representing God. Warner White, an Episcopal priest, writes on the symbolic role. He comments on how little he often does for folk who are ill: inquire about health, pray, anoint.

> Yet they often react with immense gratitude and admiration. . . . I swell inside. I have a sense of great power, of being bigger than life. . . . I also have a sense of unreality. I'm just me. What I've done is very ordinary, and yet they are reacting as if it were very extraordinary.[11]

At such times, people react to the priest-as-symbol.

This idealization of the pastor as divine symbol is especially strong early in a new pastorate; we are often seduced by such projections early in ministry. The longer one stays in a parish and the more opportunities the parish has to see one's humanity, the more possible it becomes that people will relate to one not only as a symbol. Then they might fawn over and adore other pastors, other symbols.

When I preach at other churches, parishioners there sometimes complain to me about *their* pastor. They may not realize that it is easy to preach better away from one's parish: One can polish and refine a recycled sermon, and the message is not loaded with the connotations and agenda that one often reads into messages from a pastor who is familiar. Once a woman even said to me, "I wish you were my pastor." I calmly responded: "You have an excellent pastor." That ended the conversation!

According to White, the symbol never entirely disappears. The priest-as-symbol is always in operation to some degree. The inevitable tension between the priest as symbol and the priest as human is among the most difficult problems facing pastors and parishes. Moving beyond honeymoon idealization or adoration can be painful and difficult for pastor and parishioner alike. We do well to be cautious.

Normally, pastor and parish move through three stages: honeymoon-adoration, disillusion-disappointment, and respect-esteem.[12] Each stage can take a year or two, and each stage involves increasingly accurate perceptions. Of course, pastors often respond to parishes with a parallel sequence of attitudes. One hazard for pastors is departure when a church is mired in the disappointment stage. Another hazard is a situation in which parishioners remain disillusioned, never moving beyond that stage.

Friedman notes that less-differentiated families (a term to be examined later) are "more likely to produce members who are quick to adore or be easily hurt by the clergy. They are more likely to deify (or crucify) their leaders."[13] Most clergy prefer being deified to being crucified, but both congregational attitudes show an unhealthy overfocus on the pastor.

The pastor-as-symbol poses many hazards for difficult behavior. Recall Aesop's fable about the donkey that carried an important statue in a religious procession. The donkey ("ass" might be the better term here!) was pleased that many people bowed or curtsied as he passed. He swelled up with pride and finally decided to stop moving so that he could bask in the adulation. His master struck him, reminding him that it was not the donkey himself but the *image* he carried that received the honor. "Fools claim for themselves the respect [or projection] that is given to their office."[14]

Pastor's Idealism

Not only parishioners get derailed by symbolism and high ideals. I, like many pastors, entered ministry full of idealism and high hopes. Those are good. After all, one would hardly want pastoral candidates to enter with cynicism and disillusion. But idealism also needs to change if we are to grow.

I came to the vocation of pastor through the "back door." I attended seminary because of interest in social issues and pursued a master's degree in peace studies. I did not intend to be a pastor. (My wife still reminds me that I said before we married that I would not be a pastor!) I had several friends at seminary who issued similar denials. Within a few years, most of us were pastors. Although this turn of events felt unexpected, we should not have been surprised: After all, what else were we likely to become after getting master's degrees from a seminary!

While there are advantages to the route by which God made me a pastor, there are disadvantages too. My prophetic edge was overdeveloped. With training in social analysis, it is easy to critique and criticize church institutions. Critique and criticism are important and even vital at times. But they need to be a later resort, seldom a first or early resort. This lesson took me a long time to learn.

In *Life Together*, martyred German theologian Dietrich Bonhoeffer warns against forming churches from "wish dreams." He calls it "God's grace" when idealistic dreams are shattered.[15] The problem comes, according to Bonhoeffer, when we become more attached to our ideals and

dreams than to reality. He goes so far as to declare that "God hates vision-
ary dreaming." Dreamers may become proud, judging, pretentious, self-
righteous crusaders. We become demanding of God, others, and ourselves.
While many are disappointed by disillusionment (and often angry at those
who seem to be the cause it), Bonhoeffer *welcomes* disillusion!

> The very hour of disillusionment with my brother [or sister] be-
> comes incomparably salutary, because it so thoroughly teaches
> me that neither of us can ever live by our own words and deeds,
> but only by that one Word and Deed which really binds us to-
> gether—the forgiveness of Jesus Christ.

In comments especially appropriate for those contending with difficult behavior, Bonhoeffer warns against complaining about one's church, either to
others or to God.

When tempted to complain, he says, one's first duty is self-examination
"to see whether the trouble is not due to his [or her] wish dream that should
be shattered by God; and if this be the case, let him [or her] thank God for
. . . this predicament." Bonhoeffer commends a cardinal rule of ministerial
leadership: examine yourself first.

My approach to ministry used to involve projecting all the things I felt a
church should do and be and then noting how my particular charge fell
short. This was an exercise in perpetual frustration for both me and my
congregations! A further complication: What I might demand of a congregation when I was in my 20s is different now that I am middle-aged. I
anticipate that my preferences will continue to change along the way. James
Dittes, a professor of pastoral theology and psychology, says that our greatest progress as ministers happens not when our dreams and visions are
fulfilled by the congregation but when they are denied, demeaned, or disregarded. Then we have the opportunity of hearing God's "call in the disruption"—a marvelous phrase.[16]

I do not argue against visions, dreams, or ideals, or against trying to
apply them. But a gentle approach is appropriate. We need to discern how
God might be leading: That direction might be very different from your
preference or mine. Similarly, we need to discover the particular gifts of our
local congregation. Those gifts might not fit your preferences, but they might
nevertheless signal the appropriate place to focus your energies.

I have served my present congregation long enough to move through
the honeymoon-adoration and disillusion-disappointment stages. On the

whole, we regard each other more honestly and realistically with esteem, respect, and affection. It took me a long while to recognize the special gifts in our congregation. My lack of recognition may have been due to my slowness to recognize the *importance* of those gifts.

Finally, a newcomer helped me see. She moved often and had been part of several churches. About a year after she became involved in our congregation she had a painful accident that laid her up for some time, first in the hospital and then at home. She felt overwhelmed by the care and attention she received from people in the church: "I never experienced anything like this from a church before."

I realized that caring is an important part of our giftedness and ministry. I should have recognized it earlier. People in our congregation have faced many tragedies, and time and again the church rallied in impressive ways. A nine-year-old's death, resulting from severe heart defects, was the hardest thing I had ever faced as a pastor. Yet my work was enhanced by the church's overwhelming response to this tragedy. The way the congregation rallied to one family's grief was a great ministry, not to be written off by any self-appointed prophet of what other great things an "ideal" church might accomplish.

Ministers are not going to get far with churches if all they do is offer prophetic critique. Our critiques may be pertinent or important, but they may also be our own *projections* or have more to do with our own needs. People need to hear first that we love, esteem, and value them. When we can offer genuine affirmations, then we may also be able to encourage new directions of growth and challenge.

Once my primary question as a pastor was asking how God wanted me to bring change to the church. That question is still important, but now I prefer to take a prayerful stance toward the congregation and its parishioners. I trust that God is at work among them already, was at work among them long before I got there, and will continue to work with them once I go. Now I ponder such questions as this: "What is God doing and saying here already and how can I assist?"

Triangulation

Earlier we saw how triangles function. Triangles pose special hazards for pastors. Pastors are targets for triangulation, since we are closely bound up with people's family systems and are sometimes on the receiving end of unresolved family issues. An unfinished family agenda is often displaced into the church sphere.

Sometimes parishioners try to get pastors to take sides in conflicts, whether in families or elsewhere. When I was a teenager, my father became disillusioned with our church. He built a row of greenhouses for a church elder, and that elder did not pay. Up to that time, this was the biggest business loss my father had ever endured. He appealed to the church and met with the pastor and another elder.

The pastor seemed sympathetic: "If we call a spade a spade, then that elder is a crook." But nothing more happened. My father was disillusioned—first by being ill-used by an elder and second because the church did not intervene.

When I remember this story, I still recall my father's pain. But I also remember an odd story in Luke 12:13-15 and wonder whether our pastor perhaps acted wisely. There, Jesus asks: "Who set me to be a judge or arbitrator over you?"

In the passage, Jesus is teaching about how the Holy Spirit supplies needs in times of tribulation. He is approached by a man who is in conflict with his brother over an inheritance. The placement of this incident itself is striking: a man asking Jesus for help in a crude fight about money! Back then, as now, inheritance divisions often caused disputes. (We see hints of such disputes in the Parable of the Prodigal Son.) Rabbis were sometimes asked to settle legal and family disputes.

Jesus, however, does not deal with this conflict, settle the legal question, resolve the division-of-goods debate, or take sides. He brushes off this chance to show the wisdom of Solomon: "Who set me to be a judge or arbitrator over you?" Warning against greed, he tells the Parable of the Rich Fool and teaches about materialism and anxiety. He dismisses the brothers' concerns, since materialism and wealth are spiritual hazards. Opposing the covetousness beneath the conflict, he refuses involvement. Later in this chapter, he advises avoiding the courtroom in words that also apply here: "Why do you not judge for yourselves what is right?" (Luke 12:57). Jesus advises settling out of court.

Placing this incident before teachings on greed, materialism, and covetousness shows that this is a cautionary tale, a warning. But verses 12:57ff also indicate that there is more to be gleaned from Jesus' troubling question.

In this memorable question, "Who set me to be a judge or arbitrator over you?," Jesus calls all to be *responsible*. Rather than take everything to a "higher court," whether Jesus, God, or human jurisdictions (12:57ff.), we are encouraged to work things out directly. Jesus refused to be triangulated. While Jesus seems to avoid the Solomonic option, actually Solomon also maneuvered the two mothers into solving their own problem.

I am not sure how I would respond to my father's problem now. Pastors are often asked to take sides in disputes. We do no one favors when we treat them as immature and do not allow them to work out their own problems. My father's problem seemed to be one of justice. (I heard only his side.) But ideal conflict resolution is for *both* parties to work things out together, possibly with the help of an able third party. A ruling from "on high" often does not produce a just reconciliation.

As a pastor, I have seen injustices in congregations. Sometimes I intervened, sometimes not. Sometimes intervention helped; sometimes it made things worse. The greatest healing and resolution came about when two parties willingly entered into reconciliation. (Years later this elder's son reconciled with my father: He bought another series of greenhouses at an inflated price to pay the old debt.) Jesus invites responsible behavior.

Trying to involve pastors in conflicts often parallels sibling rivalry. Siblings fight, possibly to gain or compete for parental attention. Insecurely fearing that a parent loves one more than the other, children hope that if a parent resolves a fight their way, that is as good as having the parent say that one is well-loved or perhaps even better-loved. Thus people fight over inheritance: It can symbolize parental affection and regard.

Similarly in church conflicts, some are insecure in relationships and worry that others might have better standing. Sometimes we pick fights. We hope the other will give in and be like us, thus reinforcing our hope that we might be right. (Much evangelism also comes from the unhealthy motive of reinforcing ourselves by converting others.) Or we hope to get decisive action that shows others to be in the wrong, thus bolstering our weak egos.

Early in one pastorate, people on both sides of an old conflict (sincere and faithful Christians all) told me: "If you do not take our side, I will leave." I refused, and some left. My reasons were many. Healing takes patience, prayer, and long discussions, not a ruling "from above." If people do not like rulings "from above," they can turn on the judge or arbitrator. The Hebrews criticized Moses in an ironic prefiguring of Jesus' question: "Who made you a ruler and judge over us?" (Exod. 2:14). I knew that both sides needed care and love, not being judged guilty or ruled the victor in a debilitating conflict.

Seeing God on "our side" is immature and infantile. German Protestant pastor-theologian Martin Niemöller is reported to have said: "I have learned that God is not the enemy of my enemies. God is not even the enemy of God's enemies." Just as parents can love all their children deeply and passionately without loving one more than the other, God loves and cares for us all and wants the salvation of all. God is not a judge who compares, divides, ranks, and rates us. God is a judge who examines our hearts and speaks to us directly about what ails us. God encourages us not to judge, criticize, write off, or demean others. Pastors likewise do well to avoid easily taking sides in disputes.

The worst errors I made as a pastor were in too easily taking sides when I leapt to the conclusion that someone was being oppressed or persecuted. My family of origin has deeply ingrained habits of triangling. Typically, many triangles break down into three roles: "victim," "persecutor," and "rescuer." In my extended family, someone might become a "persecutor" by acting out (anger, alcohol abuse, verbal abuse, depression, overwork), and someone else would consequently suffer as "victim." A more responsible or stable member of the family would be expected to intervene as "rescuer," forcefully persuading the "persecutor" to behave.

An oldest child, I was groomed to be a "rescuer." I took this mode into the church and into a prophetic style of pastoring. While prophetic advocacy is appropriate at times, I learned to be suspicious of my urges to rush into that mode. It took me a long time to recognize and accept the truth of what a counselor once told me: "Unfulfilled personal needs are often a contributing factor to those who act like prophets."

It is important for pastors to do family-of-origin work to realize how extensively early family life contributes to our behavior, instincts, and automatic responses. It is not only parishioners but also pastors who bring an unresolved family agenda to church issues.

There is one other reason to beware of being triangled: The game often backfires. Roles can switch. One who intervenes as "rescuer" is often perceived as "persecutor"; the "victim" and the former "persecutor" may ally against the "rescuer." Church consultant Roy Oswald noticed this tendency particularly in small churches of up to 50 members. Such churches usually have a "matriarch" or "patriarch," as well as a common hazard:

> Clergy should watch out for the trap set when members complain to them about the patriarch or matriarch of the parish and encourage the pastor to take the parental figure on. Clergy who respond to such mutinous bids, expecting the congregation to back them in the showdown, betray their misunderstanding of the dynamics of small-church ministry.[17]

If the pastor does anything about these complaints, it is likely that he or she will be abandoned by the group and attacked by the matriarch or patriarch!

That ancient guide for monasteries, *The Rule of St. Benedict*, also recognizes the dangers of triangling. Benedict is firmly opposed. Chapter 69 sternly warns:

> Every precaution must be taken that one monk does not presume . . . to defend another in the monastery or to be his champion, even if they are related by the closest ties of blood. In no way whatsoever shall the monks presume to do this, because it can be a most serious source and occasion of contention. Anyone who breaks this rule is to be *sharply restrained.*[18]

Benedict obviously considers such behavior a serious threat to the well-being of community.

While pastors need to be concerned about hurting and vulnerable people in congregations, there are wiser ways of handling potential triangles.

- First, we can encourage people to deal directly with any they regard as "persecutors."
- Second, if they are reluctant, some coaching might be in order.
- Third, failing that, one might accompany and help make dialogue possible.

We need to learn that the "greater good" of the church is not primarily our responsibility. Hurts are going to happen, and we cannot heal or resolve them all. Sometimes we can do no more than lend a caring and sympathetic ear.

Pastors' "Total Institution" Mentality

Early in my ministry, I went through a time of depression and anger which I attributed to loneliness. I blamed the church for my loneliness. Parishioners were uninterested in socializing. No one in the church took care of my needs when one of my parents faced cancer. I lived under the illusion that the church was there to meet my needs and that I had no options outside the congregation for addressing my very real concerns.

While one might be tempted to attribute responsibility for difficult behavior elsewhere, we have seen that pastors also contribute to these hazards through their own countertransference, complicity in projections, triangulation, etc.

Pastors do well to consider another possible hazard for difficult behavior. In a fascinating article on why clergy cross sexual boundaries, Princeton pastoral theology professor Donald Capps refers to a 1961 study by sociologist Erving Goffman on "total institutions": prisons, detention centers, health-care facilities, monasteries, nursing homes. Total institutions constitute an inmate's complete reality: Inmates have no life beyond them.[19]

Capps's twist is to suggest that churches function as "total institutions" for pastors. But we are not the staff in these "total institutions." Rather our work in the parish may parallel the life of an *inmate* in a prison or a mental asylum!

> Pastors often complain that they have no life *outside* the parish, that the parish consumes their every waking hour and not infrequently interrupts their sleeping hours as well. Pastors often complain that they have no time for their families and their families complain that they are frequently coopted by the church, that they, too, are not allowed to have a private life outside the parish. . . . [B]y and large, the parish functions as a total institution for the pastor, and, in that sense, the pastor's personal situation is akin to that of the patient in a long-term care hospital or the inmate in a prison, in spite of the fact that the pastor "works for" the parish and is therefore, in terms of social organizational structure, comparable to the hospital or prison staff.

Capps contends that parishioners have more in common with staff of institutions, as they can come and go. Most parishioners "have a life" or the option of "having a life" outside the church. But patients and inmates have no life outside the institution and have no choice but to be overinvolved.

When pastors experience parishes as total institutions, they feel powerless. Capps suspects that this factor contributes to the way some pastors "might begin to act out the role of 'patient' or 'inmate,' viewing themselves as 'powerless to resist' a parishioner's sexual advances (or even misrepresenting the parishioner as the one who initiated the affair)." This theory also explains why pastors so often have affairs with parishioners (when it might seem safer to have an affair "outside").

> If . . . the parish functions as a total institution for the pastor, then it is not surprising that the pastor would not go outside the parish to find someone with whom to have an affair, for, in a very real sense, the parish *is* the pastor's world, and parishioners are, in that sense, the only ones who are truly available.

It is not our purpose here to consider why pastors cross boundaries, but this metaphor of "total institution" is relevant. We need to pay attention to the possibility of a total-institution mentality.

There have been times when our family life centered on the church. When I changed pastoral assignments, it was more than changing jobs. It felt as if we were uprooting our whole life. Even now, as an introvert, I often expend so much of my socializing energies during worship, at meetings, in counseling sessions, and at church events that little energy or time is left for socializing and "having a life" outside church.

One issue is self-care and maintaining appropriate balance in one's life. But more than that, if pastors perceive themselves to be in total institutions, we may *overestimate* the seriousness of what is happening. For one, we often do not have the benefit (unless we go out of our way for it) of an outside perspective. For another, if the local congregation is our life, then the stakes will seem all the higher. If we feel a threat of losing our position, it is not just our job that hangs in the balance but our whole world, our "total institution."

Total-institution dynamics remind us to be cautious in how we interpret what strikes us as difficult.

Chronic Anxiety

It is appropriate for churches to have unhealthy people. "Those who are well have no need of a physician, but those who are sick" (Mark 2:17). But churches do not just include and embrace unhealthy people, nor do they strive unreservedly to heal the ill or bring maturity to the immature. Churches are often special havens and arenas where the immature or highly anxious act out. While anxiety is normal, high anxiety is destructive and harmful.

There are two kinds of anxiety: acute and chronic.[20]

Acute anxiety is situational, sparked by crises or irritations. It is temporary, and sooner or later we regain control over it. Budget problems, building programs, and the departure of a much-loved or little-loved pastor often cause anxiety. If that is all that goes on, then anxiety might be acute. It must be managed, but it does not necessarily reflect lack of health.

Chronic anxiety, however, is perpetual, ongoing, and habitual. Because it never ends, it is particularly problematic. Anxiety is meant to function as an alarm or warning signal, but *chronic* anxiety keeps "crying wolf." Groups, including church families, can be chronically anxious. Congregations that have the reputation of being "difficult" are usually highly anxious. Individuals too can be chronically anxious. Chronically anxious people are easily hurt, quick to complain of being victims, and sometimes quick to sue. They are unable to control their own reactivity.[21]

Peter Steinke notes that chronic anxiety is often reflected in *willfulness*: my way or else. The chronically anxious have a low pain threshold and try to rid themselves of the pain by blaming or even persecuting others.

> It is the chronically anxious individuals in the church family who are apt to conduct a "search and destroy mission." They will not hesitate to impose their wills on others. They make hostages of their gifts, attendance, and participation. They employ their stewardship as brinkmanship. Their ultimate threat is to run away from home—transferring or terminating their membership if an action is not rescinded, a person is not removed, or a demand is not satisfied.[22]

Chronically anxious people behave rigidly and habitually and cannot adjust behavior or relationships appropriately to the situation. In common jargon we call such people "stuck" and might even recommend that they "get a life." They seem unable to let go of matters that appear minor. They are unable to respond with creativity, flexibility, imagination, or innovation to challenging circumstances.

Social Incompetence

Psychiatrist and best-selling author Daniel Goleman provides another framework for understanding troubling and unsettling behavior in his discussion of social incompetence.[23] Social incompetents lack social graces, sometimes annoyingly so. These inadequate social graces can be seemingly minor: for example, not knowing how or when to end a conversation, speaking only about oneself, not paying attention to signals to change the topic of conversation, being rudely curious. Says Goleman: "These derailments of a smooth social trajectory all bespeak a deficit in the rudimentary building blocks of interaction."

Social incompetence is a theme in an episode of the popular TV situation comedy "Seinfeld." Elaine's latest boyfriend has no sense of personal space when conversing with others: he stands so close to people that he speaks directly into their mouths, never noticing that others keep backing away from him into walls or over obstacles. Seinfeld complains in the same episode about people who do not know how to shake hands: hanging on too limply, not using all fingers, not knowing when to let go.

Such ineptitude may seem trivial but has consequences. Goleman notes:

> The net effect of failing to follow these rules is to create waves, to make those around us uncomfortable. The function of these rules, of course, is to keep everyone involved in a social exchange at ease; awkwardness spawns anxiety.

I can think of numerous parishioners who did not "get it." Some would not release my hand and would back me into a conversation from which I could not extricate myself. Others did not observe hygienic habits valued in our society: Their body odor or halitosis was off-putting. Some kept raising awkward and embarrassing subjects when the group clearly did not want to deal with such issues.

People often react to such incompetence with anxiety, unease, or even resentment. The resentment stems from guilt over not knowing how to respond or from feeling awkward about one's resentment of apparent trivialities. Our responsibility includes relating to socially incompetent people and not ignoring or shunning them, as groups so often do—especially groups that value niceness and propriety.

But it is not enough to "hang in" with social incompetents, because the stakes and implications are higher than awkwardness and unease. Goleman believes social incompetence is an emotional learning disability, often visible already in children.

> *Dyssemia* (from the Greek *dys-* for "difficulty" and *semes* for "signal") . . . amounts to a learning disability in the realm of nonverbal messages; about one in ten children has one or more problems in this realm. The problem can be in a poor sense of personal space, so that a child stands too close while talking or spreads their belongings into other people's territory; in interpreting or using body language poorly; in misinterpreting or misusing facial expressions by, say, failing to make eye contact; or in a poor sense of prosody, the emotional quality of speech, so that they talk too shrilly or flatly.

The consequences of social incompetence are high for children and adults: Social incompetents are often disdained, demeaned, and rejected. Goleman says:

> If children do poorly in language, people assume they are not very bright or poorly educated; but when they do poorly in the nonverbal rules of interaction, people—especially playmates— see them as "strange," and avoid them. These are the children who don't know how to join a game gracefully, who touch others in ways that make for discomfort rather than camaraderie—in short, who are "off." They . . . have failed to master the silent language of emotion, and . . . unwittingly send messages that create uneasiness.

Social ineptitude creates uneasiness and frustration not only in others. Socially incompetent children also feel frustrated. They do not communicate what they intend or achieve what they hope to accomplish. The result is a feeling of isolation and lack of control; bewildered and anxious, they often have learning difficulties. Yet children can be taught to overcome their social ineptness.

Adults often exhibit similar behavior. In one church, a new family had attended for barely a year when they began lobbying for the removal of the popular pastor: "Either he goes, or we go." Their behavior dramatically raised anxiety among parishioners, but the family missed the signals behind this anxiety. Social incompetence in a church that esteems and does not terminate pastors led to predictable results: The family left, and the pastor stayed.

Bullying, or Why Hurt People Hurt People

A large urban congregation was stymied when one of its youth began acting violently toward other youth. Confronting the situation only heightened the conflict. At one point, the teenage girl got drunk and damaged church property. The mother rose to her defense, joining a class for new members and using it as a podium to complain about how poorly the leadership had treated her daughter. The class teachers considered holding the class in secret but finally canceled it altogether.

One problematic behavior in churches is *bullying*. Goleman believes that overaggressive behavior is often closely tied to "emotionally inept parenting." Aggression is passed down through the generations: People who bully often raise others who bully. Aggressive children often have "parents who disciplined them with arbitrary, relentless severity," and they grow up to be bullying parents.[24]

> These children were disciplined capriciously: if their parents were in a bad mood, they would be severely punished; if their parents were in a good mood, they could get away with mayhem at home. Thus punishment came not so much because of what the child had done, but by virtue of how the parent felt. This is a recipe for feelings of worthlessness and helplessness, and for the sense that threats are everywhere and may strike at any time.

The emotional costs are high and the combative consequences often severely destructive, warping "a child's natural bent toward empathy," according to Goleman. Childhood aggression is often the beginning of a lifelong pattern. Even people who overcome and control their ingrained bent toward aggressiveness and combativeness may bully again in reactive moments.

Goleman shows how "these savage imprints can be mended" and describes examples of "emotional relearning" and "reeducating the emotional brain." Strategies entail long-term therapeutic work (role-playing, retelling, medication, alternating reimmersion and respite, mourning, psychotherapy).

Goleman worries that aggressiveness and combativeness are rising. Increasing violence in schools is a sign of trouble and shows our "desperate need for lessons in handling emotions, settling disagreements peaceably, and just plain getting along."

Childhood bullies resemble chronically anxious and undifferentiated persons:

> Such angry, isolated children are highly sensitive to injustices and being treated unfairly. They typically see themselves as victims and can recite a list of instances when . . . teachers blamed them for doing something when in fact they were innocent. Another trait of such children is that once they are in the heat of anger they can think of only way to react: by lashing out.

The relevance of this description is clearer when we see that Hugh Halverstadt explicitly connects aggressive, conflictive behavior in the church to childhood experiences and beliefs.[25] He believes that shame precludes people from responding with mature assertion.

> They perceive . . . conflicts as occasions when their secret defectiveness will be found out. Therefore, shame-based parties experience conflicts as occasions when they must prove to be right at whatever cost. They are literally driven to be right.
>
> Their goal in conflicts is to be a winner, so as to seem superior. Their terror is to be a loser, which they perceive as being defective.

This perception leads to unthinking, reactive, automatic behavior, and the implications are sobering. Says Halverstadt:

The only way shame-based antagonists know to resolve conflicts is to determine who is right or wrong, good or bad. They cannot resolve issues without judging persons. Nor can they accept or offer compromises without feeling that they are acknowledging imperfections that might expose their defectiveness. Such tormented parties are often major players in chronically destructive church conflicts.

Goleman calls such behavior a "jump to judgment": "Once they assume threat, they leapfrog into action." The more people react to quickly perceived hostility with aggression, the more automatic this response becomes. Such people may actually know no other way!

Goleman discusses the low thresholds that such folk have for getting upset. He describes ways of overcoming automatic hostility. Emotional competence can be taught and coached, even if not all emotional disorders can be overcome.

When we recognize what lies behind disruptive and difficult behavior, we may not be so quick to judge or to write off such behavior as "sin" that simply needs to be reprimanded by "us" and repented of by "them." Rather, our understanding first gives us some empathy for what others face. We also have a better sense of what is required in response. "It is truly said that hurt people hurt people."[26]

Assessment is crucial. In Halverstadt's system of managing conflict, a crucial step is determining whether those involved in the conflict are likely to fight "dirty" or "fair."[27] The purpose of assessment is appraisal and responsible decision-making.

CHAPTER 4

Hardball and Softball: Unhealthy Responses

There will always be difficult behavior in church. Our previous chapter gives us handles for understanding and assessing such behavior and taking a "research stance" toward it. We can neither change nor avoid the inevitable reality of difficult behavior. Therefore, what should we do? How can we respond? Ignoring or avoiding such problems does not help. They do not go away; often they get worse.

Many resources on handling conflict are useful. But dealing with difficult behavior is a more specific problem within the larger issue of conflict management. Conflict-management approaches help us to see that there are primarily two unhealthy extremes in dealing with difficult behavior in the congregation.

Adversarial "Hardball" as an Unhealthy Reaction

One unhealthy extreme, the "fight" modes of response, can be categorized as blame, retribution, hostility, and counterattack. Retaliatory adversarialism usually fails,

> although it can be quite effective in releasing anger for the moment. But the newly compounded problem produces even more future anxiety. Although many church leaders have tried, it is difficult to win a battle against someone causing conflict within a church. Even if the leader wins a battle, it rarely means that the war has ended.[1]

Difficult behavior should not be resisted with difficult behavior. Many self-help books recommend counterattacks: Such tactics may not be as adversarial as the precipitating behavior, but their goal is basically to outwit, subvert, outmaneuver, or silence opponents. "Hardball" and counterattacks are essentially reactive. Friedrich Nietzsche is said to have warned: "[One] who fights with monsters might take care lest [one] thereby become a monster."

Psychiatrist and best-selling author M. Scott Peck believes that adversarial responses happen in a quick three-step process.[2] First, responsibility for tension is attributed to another. Second, the other is blamed for acting from "malicious or even insane motives." Finally, adversarial processes are used. "Ninety-five percent of the time it is unconscious, uncivil, and unnecessary."

Peck shows that all three steps are faulty, inadequate, and harmful. First, as systems thinking shows, the presenting problem is often not the real issue. Second, blaming is likely to be a "rush to judgment." We are not able to read the motives of others. A rush to judgment is tempting because it means less work and perhaps less self-scrutiny. In his study on forced terminations of pastors, Speed Leas notes that the most common problem with pastors' behavior during termination is their moving to unethical and punitive acts: "attacking people by saying to them or others that they are mentally ill, calling them names, impugning their reputations, or putting them down in order to make them feel bad."[3]

While not many people *advocate* adversarial responses, it is a temptation. In rare instances, asking people to leave might be an appropriate last resort, but a risky one. From a purely pragmatic perspective, it can make apparent martyrs out of ousted opponents. Asking people to leave can cause great damage. Leas warns: "Therefore, if such action is necessary, the cost of asking persons to leave should outweigh the cost of allowing things to remain as they are."[4]

Accordingly, he says that asking individuals or small groups to leave may be appropriate if the church does not have time, energy, or ability to deal with inappropriate behavior; if many efforts have been made to communicate clear expectations of appropriate behavior; or if offenders regularly or frequently behave in abusive ways. Nevertheless, asking people to leave is the rare exception rather than the rule.

If altruistic instincts or pragmatic cautions are not enough to convince us to resist adversarialism or a crusader mentality, then we do well to heed Edwin Friedman's warning that trying to achieve change by force (or even by simple direct motivation) does not work: When leaders "push, pull, tug, kick, shove, threaten, convince, arm-twist, charm, entice, cajole, seduce, induce guilt, shout louder, or [are] more eloquent," they may or may not be successful, but "change tends to be short-lived and enervating."[5] Trying to force change tends paradoxically to reinforce the status quo.

But adversarial confrontations and overt "exorcisms" are not the only ways we seek to address debilitating behavior.

Hardball and Softball Juxtaposed

I should not have been surprised. Teaching an adult Sunday-school class, I invited the group to reflect on how our church came up short: Where were we failing to live up to the vision of the church as proclaimed in Eph. 2?

Darrell spoke up with vehemence and venom. His voice was loud: "People are not friendly! When visitors come, I'm the only one who speaks to them. If it wasn't for me, no one would speak to them at all. I think it is shameful that we are so inhospitable."

Darrell had every right, of course, to voice concerns and criticisms about our church, especially as his pastor had invited such reflections. But anxiety rose in the room during his little speech. His tone and body language conveyed deep anger. His generalizations about what others never did seemed almost too overwhelming to counter. His self-justification was unfortunate. His aggressive tone and demeanor made discussion difficult.

And, not surprisingly in our congregation, no one said a word. Darrell's concerns and objections were duly noted, and the discussion moved on to other things.

After class, Timothy, an aging newcomer, waylaid me in the classroom once everyone else had left. He told me quietly: "I want you to know that I did not agree with Darrell. People have always been friendly to me, and I feel welcome here."

I appreciated the good words from Timothy. And while as a church leader I might be biased about Darrell's criticisms, I suspected that Timothy's experience was true for him and for many other newcomers. Yet I fear that his way of dealing with conflict was as unhealthy as Darrell's.

"Softball" as an Unhealthy Reaction

Most people see that adversarial approaches are inappropriate. In a culture that values pluralism, multiculturalism, and tolerance, this recognition is not surprising. In my own ecclesiastical tradition, this view is reinforced by our own reaction to church discipline practiced by leaders early in the 20th century and our realization that it was too harsh and inflexible. We reject those "hardball" approaches, but we have, alas, fallen into an opposite extreme.

"Softball" or "flight modes" might be seen as the opposite of "hardball," but they too are problematic. Such unhealthy responses are sometimes categorized as indirect, nonconfrontational, passive, sentimental, placating, or appeasing. Both "hardball" and "softball" in fact often do more harm than good.

Some congregations and leaders downplay, ignore, or quickly ameliorate any tension. Peter Steinke notes that certain modes of difficult behavior by individuals or groups—"search and destroy missions," imposition of will, "stewardship as brinkmanship," and threats to leave—are effective tactics "in church families that place a premium on peace and harmony. They will exchange integrity for tranquillity."[6] Leas is particularly concerned about churches' unwillingness or inability to confront problems, difficulties, and grievances.

> The problem with many congregations is that efforts to "tell others their faults" are usually puny, if existent at all. People become dissatisfied, murmur among themselves, and increase their sense of frustration by complaining to themselves while doing very little to confront the sources of their difficulty.[7]

Mansell Pattison attributes some inability to confront to the way pastors are trained. Our stereotype of pastoral care as being "purely passive, nondirective, and value-free" is influenced by "client-centered" psychologist Carl Rogers. While Pattison has a high regard for Rogerian approaches, he says a pastor must be more than nondirective "because he or she represents the reliable values, commitments, standards, and behavior patterns established by the church."[8]

We do no one a favor by neglecting to point chronically anxious people toward more responsible behavior.

> Governed by instinct rather than insight, [chronically anxious people] cannot be stopped by reasoning or appeasing. Mistakenly, those who must deal with them think being "nice" to the chronically anxious will earn cooperation in return. Or that being reasonable will get the reactive forces to follow suit.[9]

Not so! Steinke asserts that being gentle does not solve the problems. Chronically anxious people do "not respond to nice behavior, clear thought, or sugar and roses," and "thoughtful and careful approaches are ignored." He warns:

> With the chronically anxious, the contentious issue is not the basis of their reactivity. Even if the issue changes, their chimes are still ringing. They keep adding emotional fuel to the fire.

Thus he cautions against sentimental approaches to chronically anxious or difficult behavior. The major problem with difficult behavior is not so much the behavior itself, but how congregations and leaders deal with and respond to that behavior. Soft approaches to adversarial behavior show an inability to deal with the anxiety that differences, division, and differentiation provoke.

Steinke believes that our desire to be nice is a cover for our own anxiety. Consequently we give power to chronically anxious "reactors"—"the least mature, least motivated, least self-regulating, but most recalcitrant people." Paul Stevens and Phil Collins speak of "the tyranny of the weak," noting that "many emotionally and spiritually weak people do dominate the church."[10] Thus, as Friedman notes: "In system after system, it is the most dependent who are calling the shots."[11] This is an unhealthy picture indeed.

Such folk could not command power in churches if they were not *given* it. Difficult behavior has power when others enable it. *We* act this way when we rush to soothe or solve the pain of others, but that rush to soothe or solve also tells us something about ourselves. And it does not work.

> Rather than facing off against each other, people make trade-offs. The reactive [members] . . . are treated with "kid gloves" or the "soft shoe." Nevertheless, sentimentalism is as reactive as

pugilism. Many churches like to fight emotional fires with sprin-
kling cans. Preferring "homey togetherness," they are cautious to
avoid, as much as possible, hard feelings or hurt feelings. Senti-
mentalists, having low toleration of pain, cannot see that they are
mistaking appeasing for loving. Further, they cannot recognize
that their empathy is related more to their own need to be relieved of their anxiety in the presence of pain than to genuine
care for the hurting.[12]

While we might think we act this way for the benefit of others or for the
good of the church, actually we do it for ourselves.

We often overlook the futility of this approach, Steinke notes:

> Sentimentalists seldom realize that reactors have "holes in their
> buckets." They are poor containers. No matter how much ground
> you give, how many peace proposals you offer, or what sound
> reasons you present, it is to no advantage. What is given in care is
> not received or appreciated. It leaks out as quickly as water from
> a bucket with holes. More will be expected. Meanwhile the reac-
> tors are not held responsible for their actions and are shielded
> from challenge. Consequently they continue to function so that
> others will take care of them, comfort them, and surrender to
> their emotional bargaining. In turn, sentimentalists . . . give and
> give, sacrificing their own integrity and sustaining the reactivity
> of the anxious.[13]

In trying to address our own low tolerance of pain, we sacrifice ourselves
and our perspectives as well. Health does not result. Such approaches respect neither others nor ourselves: There is no mutual benefit.

Steinke ties this sacrifice to the Golden Calf story in Exod. 32.

> Aaron is too sensitive to the people's pain. He wants only to re-
> lieve their incessant, nagging complaints. But Moses is on a quest
> for truth. He will not heal the people's pain with some narcotic or
> magic. "The reason, by the way," Friedman mentions, "that Moses
> has a higher threshold for his people's pain than Aaron is because
> Moses has vision."[14]

Friedman warns against quickly relieving pain, as tempting as that may be, because "the quicker leaders (or therapists) are to relieve their followers' pain, the less real change they will bring to the system."[15]

Church consultant Gil Rendle illustrates the hazards nicely in a homey metaphor.

> Trying to make everyone happy is like stepping into a shower too quickly on a chilly morning. We instinctively reach for the hot water and turn it up hoping to fix the problem, but end up unbalancing the system. The shower then becomes too hot because we have overattended to the hot water. We then have to reach for the cold, often in the process further unbalancing the system and requiring that we play with the faucets a third or fourth time. The more you play with the faucets, trying to "fix" the water temperature, the longer the system stays in disequilibrium.
>
> So . . . trying to satisfy each and every demand in the congregation . . . does not lead to improvement, or even satisfaction of the complaints. It simply keeps the system out of balance and in a reactive mode as various expectations compete.[16]

Are There Other Options?

As much as I love and admire my cats, I am not impressed with their intellect. A neighbor cat likes to stroll through our yard. Our cats find this encroachment on their turf offensive enough. But what really drives them crazy is another habit of the neighbor cat. He walks up to the patio window and stares into the house. Our cats, hair raised and fat-tailed, go ballistic: meowing and crying, jumping against the window, hissing and spitting.

The other cat sits there, apparently calm, not budging an inch. The longer he stays, the angrier our cats become. The irony is that their highly anxious behavior changes nothing except their own state of mind. They cannot do or change anything through the glass. The issue is really not that important, as the neighbor cat is not touching them. Furthermore, if they happened to be in another room, they would never know that he was there.

Reactivity in churches (both hardball and softball) is usually no more helpful than my cats' behavior. In fact, it is often *harmful* to ourselves and others. We have seen the demerits and dangers of two common responses to difficult behavior and adversarialism: failing to respond appropriately or overreacting. Are there other alternatives?

In an important book on leadership, Ronald A. Heifetz, a Harvard University professor, suggests that social systems have three alternatives when seeking equilibrium after disequilibrium.[17]

First, organizations may rely on their accustomed repertoire of responses. As we have seen, churches often choose either "hardball" or "softball" approaches. Both are generally ineffective, reactive, and irresponsible. One aphorism suggests: Insanity is doing the same thing over and over but expecting different results.

Second, systems may use the responses within their repertoire for the sake of achieving short-term peace and short-range solutions. This option, like "hardball" and "softball" approaches, ignores long-term consequences and responsibility.

A third option is to learn new responses to the challenges, addressing problems in ways that solve issues and address underlying problems. Heifetz calls this "adaptive work."

People fail to adapt for a number of reasons. They may not realize the seriousness of the threat. Some people in the pew do not take problems of difficult behavior seriously. Sometimes systems see the threat but find the challenge too big; a controversy explodes, and people simply do not know how to respond. They may panic, hope the problem will go away, or find themselves too exhausted and depleted to deal with the issue at hand.

Steinke notes that when churches are faced with "collective stressors," they can go in one of two directions. They can either go the route of "*eustress* (promoting health) or *distress* (enabling disease)."[18]

One snowy morning I drove the high school car pool. I backed the fully loaded van onto a downwardly sloped street. On the slippery pavement, the van would not budge uphill in a forward gear. I could have pushed the accelerator, spun the wheels harder and faster, and gotten nowhere. Instead, I backed partway down the hill, tried the forward gear again, discovered my wheels had found a purchase, and was able to move forward. That was adaptive work.

So far, we have given plenty of attention to *distress*, both difficult behavior that plagues churches and the ways churches enable that behavior. It is now time to explore the *eustress* of adaptive work.

CHAPTER 5

Turkeys and Burning Barns

One of my parishioners has a turkey farm. According to him, turkeys deserve their reputation for not being too bright.

Once a turkey barn caught on fire. The turkeys huddled together in a corner. When the farmer opened the barn door to allow the turkeys to escape the danger, they refused to move. So the farmer entered the barn and shooed them out the door. Initially, they cooperated. But then they circled the perimeter of the barn until they found a hole in the wall. Then they plunged right back into the barn's familiar confines![1]

Since I argue against name-calling, I would not want to say that churches or church people are turkeys! But our reliance on old, familiar methods of dealing with difficult behavior has left us in a rut. Rather than act like turkeys roosting in a burning barn, we need to find healthy responses to difficult behavior.

Respect, Empathy, Challenge, and Concern

We have seen that churches often respond to difficult behavior in ways that perpetuate or reinforce problems, either with "hardball" (rigid, unyielding, inflexible, and harsh approaches) or "softball" (yielding, enabling, and naïve reactions). The challenge is to find a way of "eustress"—a firmness that the avoids pitfalls of both "softball" and "hardball": flexible but not floppy, compassionate but not "sloppy agape," steady but not immovable.

Part of the problem is an inadequate view of *reconciliation*. We sometimes believe that the Christian imperative of reconciliation (2 Cor. 5:20-21) means avoiding confrontation at all costs, forgoing prophetic advocacy, and accommodating irresponsibility. Reconciliation need not be *resignation*.

One challenge is to find *respectful* ways of responding to difficult behavior. Adversarial methods demean or write off others. But soft approaches are also problematic in that they respect neither the other's responsibility nor our own point of view.

Another challenge is to find responses that show concern and empathy. Adversarial methods lose sight of the individual and the pain that such methods bring to difficult situations. Again, soft approaches exhibit misplaced empathy, a "sloppy agape" that does not invite growth. Part of the problem is our tendency to avoid or eliminate both tension and conflict. Yet both are normal and healthy in relationships.

Another clue to dealing responsibly with difficult behavior comes from pastoral counseling. Misplaced empathy deters people from confrontation, but in pastoral counseling empathy and confrontation are integrally related: they evoke and build on each other, and each needs the other.

To respond to disturbing behavior with either "fight" or "flight" is emotionally immature and avoids professional obligations. Neither shows sufficient regard, respect, or empathy for the other. Thus Conrad Weiser commends *concern,* which includes a desire to help and a commitment not to damage.[2] Both sides of this equation are important. It is not enough to avoid damage; wanting only to help can encourage immaturity in the other. Concern entails both connection and distance. Once again we deal with a "both/and" pair that some consider opposites, moving beyond excessive distance (withdrawal) or excessive involvement (acting out). Systems thinkers pose a dual challenge to leaders: to be nonanxiously differentiated from others but remaining in contact with them. The notion of concern embraces both dimensions.

Hugh Halverstadt also affirms the importance of reconciliation, respect, empathy, concern, and challenge when he advocates a Christian ethic of responsible assertiveness. For him, three behavioral standards are essential: personal assertiveness, respect for others' rights, and sharing assertiveness for common good.[3]

Many Christians are suspicious of assertiveness; they may take seriously Jesus' recommendation in the Sermon on the Mount of "turning the other cheek." Some Christians hesitate to speak their mind. But this does not mean that they abandon their convictions or concerns! Rather they deal with them indirectly through sabotage, subterfuge, grapevines, passive-aggressiveness, gossip, or triangulation.

Jesus consistently exemplified assertiveness with both friends and foes.

Halverstadt says assertiveness is the healthiest way to achieve another tricky "both/and," *love of neighbor as well as self.*

> To love oneself in place of others is aggression or manipulation. Aggression/manipulation sacrifices others for one's ends. To love others in place of oneself is passivity. Passivity sacrifices oneself for others' ends. To love others as oneself is assertiveness. Assertiveness recognizes a common intrinsic worth to all parties and calls for self-investment rather than self-sacrifice. Christian assertiveness leads us into struggles of giving to and giving with others rather than giving up or giving in to others.[4]

Halverstadt's second element of Christian assertiveness requires *interpersonal respect*, balancing respect of others with respect of self. This element honors the second half of the great commandment: loving others as we love ourselves.

His third crucial element of responsible Christian assertiveness is *sharing a goal for the common good*. Personal assertiveness is not enough, as it can lead to self-centered preoccupation. Personal assertiveness and interpersonal respect are not enough, as they can become so preoccupied with the personal relationship that the good of the group is overlooked. Here we look at the big picture of God's intention for the wider good.

One pastor, who often included chancel dramas in worship, embodied respect and confrontation in handling a parishioner's complaints and unhappiness. An older member, accustomed to old ways and styles, could never adjust to the notion that dramas had an appropriate place in worship. He complained loudly and often. Finally, the pastor came up with a solution. She telephoned this older man before any worship service that would include a drama to warn him of what was coming. Thus alerted, he could opt out of attending any service with a drama. He never complained about dramas again. And he never missed a service either!

A Sense of Coherence

When faced with difficult behavior in a congregation, it is essential that leaders assess the health or lack thereof brought to any particular conflict. Peter Steinke concludes that individual and group wellness or illness, healing or deterioration, has to do with *a sense of coherence*:

a disposition or orientation to life: all the parts of one's life are connected, something ties all people together, and life coheres in a meaningful way. This sense of coherence gives people a compass, builds confidence that the person can positively influence the outcome.[5]

In the face of challenges and stressors, a sense of coherence makes a major difference in whether the group can respond in a healthy way. Steinke names three ingredients. First, *meaningfulness:* A congregation believes its actions have meaning and worth. Second, *manageability:* A congregation believes it has some control and influence over outcomes. Third, *comprehensibility:* The congregation understands the challenges and knows how to move toward health.

If coherence is strong, the group can be realistic and less anxious when facing, dealing with, assessing, and responding to conflict and difficult behavior. As well, people are less reactive and have a broader repertoire of responses to problems they face.

Leaders need to know how their congregations stand as they try to assess what they can realistically hope for from the group.

Levels of Conflict

In the introduction, we noted that Speed Leas helpfully describes five levels of intensity of conflict: problems to solve, disagreement, contest, fight/flight, and intractable situations. Our concern with difficult behavior is confined to the latter three levels.[6]

At Level III, we encounter win/lose dynamics (rather than win/win, which are more realizable at the first two levels). At this level winning is of ultimate importance. People guard their position and their side. Their language reflects distortions: dichotomizing, universalizing, magnifying, arbitrarily inferring, deleting. Groups and coalitions may emerge. Personal attacks increase. People appeal more to emotions than to rational thinking. Parties assume they know others' motives.

At this stage, many things are possible, and many people can be encouraged to participate. Collaborative problem-solving would include mutually working at defining the problem, gathering information, searching for various solutions, and choosing the best solution. If collaboration fails, then compromise or negotiation is in order. The group should work at identifying its beliefs about conflict and should also develop fair-fighting ground rules. It is worthwhile developing common goals, history, values, and interests. Training in communication skills is in order.

At Level IV, "fight/flight," people's major goal is to break relationships: One party or the other must leave. Tactics can include attacks with the purpose of weakening or causing hurt or humiliation. Factions begin to emerge. Defeating the other is more important than solving the problem. Factions put their agenda at the top. The integrity of others is attacked. Attempts are made to expel others.

At such levels, it is important to recognize the authority of structures and to observe due process (rights, rules, fair play). It is appropriate to search for common goals, values, and interests. Third parties may help adversaries state and explain their positions. Once a win/lose decision is made, allow people to withdraw, separate, or leave. Stress the authority of the leadership or majority, and uphold their decisions. People who function at Level IV should not be given influential or powerful positions or high visibility (although leaders may sympathize with folk at Level IV).

At Level V, "intractable," the major goal is destruction of the "enemy." Issues are described in broad, larger-than-life strokes. People see themselves as fighting a crusade. Any means are justified. Withdrawing is worse than defeating the opponents. Leas advocates firm intervention at this point. Authorities or peacekeepers are needed to prevent antagonists from fighting. Groups may need to be separated. If people are excessively disruptive, they may have to be asked to leave.

Leas calls high-level conflict with individuals or tiny minorities among the most difficult conflicts to address. He warns against increasing the power of people in that mode: Such members should not be nominated or appointed to office. At Level IV or above,

> such individuals usually do not have the good of the organization
> first on their agenda, do not have the patience or skills (in this
> setting) to influence others appropriately, and are not trusted enough
> to engender hope on the part of others that their recommenda-
> tions and actions will be helpful.[7]

Not only must their power not be increased; it is also important to stress the authority of the leadership or majority. Here "softball" approaches are especially problematic. Leas counsels firmness rooted in due process and established authority.

If charges are made, take them seriously, investigate them, and respond appropriately (or agitation will continue). After investigation, the leadership should report one of the following: There is no problem, changes will be made accordingly, the situation was misunderstood, or no changes will be made. Dissenters need to be reminded when issues have been dealt with. Appropriate firmness is also reflected in Leas's recommendation that people "should be asked to play by the rules, the same rules by which the board and other church leaders play."

Norms of Conflicts

Leas believes that the *norms* of the group are a key factor in shaping conflicts. Norms are what family-systems theorists call "family rules."

> Norms are necessary to group life, because they are a part of the glue that holds society together. Norms are the unwritten rules that people abide by in order to function as a group. By and large, people are not fully conscious of the norms that shape their behavior, unless they are infringed upon or challenged.[8]

Norms guide us in what to do and what is appropriate. They also involve *sanctions* when a norm is violated.

Congregational norms for conflict influence how difficult behavior is handled. "Hardball" and "softball" approaches reflect unhelpful norms, especially if conflict is seen as a failure to be avoided at all costs. I see that norm often in churches. When conflict arises, people ask: "How can Christians behave this way?" Sometimes people who name conflicts or who identify abuse are resented for violating the norm of pretending that no conflicts exist. That is one reason why prophets are often not accepted in their own country, as Jesus noted.

As Leas observes, this no-conflict norm is particularly dangerous when combined with anxiety.

> When you put fear of conflict together with norms that prohibit its expression, you get a double dose of problems. This double trouble keeps the organization in turmoil longer, makes . . . members feel

less able to control themselves and their organization, and increases the likelihood of an explosion of blaming, attacking, and getting rid of.

From Halverstadt and Virginia Hoffman,[9] the latter a professor at Loyola University, Chicago, we learn norms that facilitate dirty fighting:

- Christians should not fight.
- Judging is appropriate.
- It is important to defend God, no matter how.
- Leaders are always either right or wrong.
- Say nothing if you cannot say something nice.
- Christians always sacrifice self.
- It is important to be right.
- Never compromise.
- Do not challenge the situation or discuss difficulties.
- Promote unrealistic expectations of being strong, good, right, or perfect.
- Do not try new things: "We've never done it that way before."
- Do not express feelings.
- Indirect communication is best.

Norms need to be identified by the group, and unhealthy norms need to be changed. Leaders can help groups surface and identify their norms. Then the group can make decisions about which norms are healthy and which need to be changed or discarded. People can be encouraged to discover and embrace new norms. As well, consider the sanctions used for noncompliance and make a commitment to acting on those sanctions.

Healthy Guidelines for Conflict

When I work with engaged couples in premarital counseling, they are often surprised to hear that we need to work on rules for *fair fighting*. The surprise comes in different ways. Some couples have not yet experienced much conflict and do not expect to see any. Other couples have seen substantial conflict (either between themselves or between the parents of one or the other) but are uneasy with this reality. The happiest occasion is the realization by a couple that conflict is normal and that the key to success is to find healthy ways of dealing with it.

Just as pastors can offer couples help in "fair fighting," guidelines can suggest healthy ways of dealing with conflicts in our congregations.

Halverstadt[10] is concerned about the following *destructive* behaviors:

- *Enemy-making*: perceiving, labeling, or identifying the other as an "enemy."
- *Hierarchical*: trying to control others.
- *Polarizing*: reducing issues to "black-and-white" solutions and giving little time to discovering other options.
- *Repressing*: all-or-nothing thinking that downplays or dismisses the range and diversity of perspectives.
- *Judgmental*: writing off others as inadequate or inferior.
- *Violating*: transgressing the personal boundaries of others with language, tone of voice, or body movements.
- *Adversarial*: using "we/they" language and ignoring or dismissing what is held in common.
- *Caricaturing and assaulting character*: portraying oneself in saintly light and others as despicable.
- *Misrepresenting*: conveying misleading information or misinterpretations of the actions or motivations of another.
- *Threatening:* issuing ultimatums.

It is important to have rules and guidelines for fair fighting. Halverstadt believes that fair-fight behaviors include four primary commitments and standards:[11]

- Share control of the conflict process with others. (Dirty fighting struggles for control over others.)
- Seek the common good over the interests of particular parties. (Dirty fighting seeks the good of the few at the expense of the many.)
- Act assertively in ways that respect self and others. (Dirty fighting involves aggressive, disrespectful, or manipulative behavior.)
- Act in ways that are accountable to the group and the authorities. (Dirty fighting involves deception of others.)

If these principles are too general, ground rules may need to be spelled out. It is most helpful when a group arrives at these on its own. Halverstadt offers these suggestions:[12]

- Do not label or name-call.
- Do not attack or question motives.
- Propose positive changes; do not just offer negative complaints.
- Speak specifically, not generally.
- Speak up for yourself and not for others; use "I-language."
- Consider and respect different perspectives; gather plenty of information.
- Be open about differences.
- Be responsible for your own feelings.
- Act accountable.
- Work for win-win solutions.
- Value everyone.
- Be open to change and growth.
- Stick with the process.
- Take a break when things get too heated.
- Admit mistakes.
- When the group makes a decision, comply with it.

In 1995, the General Conference Mennonite Church and the Mennonite Church General Assembly adopted a helpful document: "Agreeing and Disagreeing in Love: Commitments for Mennonites in Times of Disagreement." It could assist congregations by helping establish fair and healthy norms and guidelines.

> "Making every effort to maintain the unity of the Spirit in the bond of peace" (Ephesians 4:3), as both individual members and the body of Christ, we pledge that we shall:
>
> *In Thought*
> 1. Accept conflict: Acknowledge together that conflict is a normal part of our life in the church. Romans 14:1-8, 10-12, 17-19; 15:1-7.
> 2. Affirm hope: Affirm that as God walks with us in conflict we can work through to growth. Ephesians 4:15-16.
> 3. Commit to prayer: Admit our needs and commit ourselves to pray for a mutually satisfactory solution (no prayers for my success or for the other to change but to find a joint way). James 5:16.
>
> *In Action*
> 4. Go to the other . . . : Go directly to those with whom we disagree; avoid behind-the-back criticism. (Go directly if you are

European-North American; in other cultures disagreements are often addressed through a trusted go-between.) Matthew 5:23-24; 18:15-20.

5. . . . In the spirit of humility: Go in gentleness, patience, and humility. Place the problem between us at neither doorstep and own our part in the conflict instead of pointing out the other's. Galatians 6:1-5.

6. Be quick to listen: Listen carefully, summarize and check out what is heard before responding. Seek as much to understand as to be understood. James 1:19; Proverbs 18:13.

7. Be slow to judge: Suspend judgments, avoid labeling, end name calling, discard threats, and act in a nondefensive, nonreactive way. Romans 2:1-4; Galatians 5:22-26.

8. Be willing to negotiate: Work through the disagreements constructively. Acts 15; Philippians 2:1-11.

   • Identify issues, interests, and needs of both (rather than take positions).

   • Generate a variety of options for meeting both parties' needs (rather than defending one's own way).

   • Evaluate options by how they meet the needs and satisfy the interests of all sides (not one side's values).

   • Collaborate in working out a joint solution (so both sides gain, both grow and win).

   • Cooperate with the emerging agreement (accept the possible, not demand your ideal).

   • Reward each other for each step forward toward agreement (celebrate mutuality).

In Life

9. Be steadfast in love: Be firm in our commitment to seek a mutual solution; be stubborn in holding to our common foundation in Christ; be steadfast in love. Colossians 3:12-15.

10. Be open to mediation: Be open to accept skilled help. If we cannot reach agreement among ourselves, we will use those with gifts and training in mediation in the larger church. Philippians 4:1-3.

11. Trust the community: We will trust the community and if we cannot reach agreement or experience reconciliation, we will

turn the decision over to others in the congregation or from the broader church. Acts 15.

- In one-to-one or small group disputes, this may mean allowing others to arbitrate.
- In congregational, conference, district or denominational disputes, this may mean allowing others to arbitrate or implementing constitutional decision-making processes, insuring that they are done in the spirit of these guidelines, and abiding by whatever decision is made.

12. Be the Body of Christ: Believe in and rely on the solidarity of the Body of Christ and its commitment to peace and justice, rather than resort to the courts of law. I Corinthians 6:1-6.[13]

All such lists are suggestive, neither exhaustive nor prescriptive. Obviously many factors influence which guidelines are embraced.

Identify and develop guidelines that encourage fair fighting, and hold the group to this standard when dealing with differences. Sticking to such guidelines will go far in limiting the damage that difficult behavior can do.

The Importance of Grievance Procedures

Churches often get into hassles because they have no established grievance procedures. Where do people go when they have concerns about or even charges against leaders? To whom do they speak? What is the highest authority in the congregation? Is the administrative board responsible for the pastor's job description, employment, and evaluation? Where is the pastor held accountable? At what point does the board or the pastor invite outside help, either from the denomination or from conflict experts? Who makes these decisions? These basic questions often do not have clear answers. Thus concerned and unhappy people may escalate their activities and charges to get action or satisfaction.

After a major conflict, our church decided to establish grievance procedures. Rather than reinvent the wheel, we approached a number of churches and asked for a copy of their own grievance procedures. Unfortunately, as we quickly learned, most had none.

Leas describes a helpful grievance procedure involving dissatisfaction with pastors. His broad outline is helpful in developing appropriate guidelines.[14]

- Clearly identify specific concerns, including relevant feelings. Differentiate feelings from objective facts.
- Inform the concerned parties about issues, problems, or feelings.
- Give permission to oneself and others to change behaviors or attitudes.
- If changes are not forthcoming, take concerns to the appropriate board or committee. The party charged should hear the complaints.
- If the complaints have grounds, the responsible body should write up the concerns and give the accused a chance to respond. Response might also include a reasonable length of time to change. In that case, a trusted accountability team could work with the charged person to evaluate progress or lack thereof. The person charged might also name certain desirable changes.
- If changes do not happen or are inadequate, officials can be asked to resign. If this approach does not work, follow your church or denominational guidelines for removal.

As part of establishing a grievance procedure, it is necessary to lodge responsibility for it with a committee—personnel committee, pastor-parish relations committee, administrative board, or other appropriate group.

It is not enough to have policies and committees. It is crucial for people to observe the established process. Our grievance policies and committees can be only as effective as our willingness to enforce and uphold them.

Support/Listening/Accountability Teams

After our congregation endured a bitter conflict, we tried to formulate guidelines for dealing with conflicts in our congregation. Our conference minister, Doris Gascho, recommended forming support/listening/accountability (SLA) teams.

In certain situations, churches (possibly working with outside consultants) may appoint an SLA team to alleviate and ventilate pain that people feel because of relationship to or involvement in a conflict. The personnel of such teams is appointed by the board or by whatever group the board puts in charge of the conflict-management process. Aggrieved parties who benefit from the SLA team might be invited to suggest possible names for inclusion, but the final selection is up to the board or its designee. The group's coordinator is directly accountable to the board or its designee.

A major function of this group is to listen and care. Thus all members need to be good listeners. This would then be the agreed forum for aggrieved parties to air complaints. As appropriate, the SLA team holds aggrieved parties accountable for behaving according to the church's agreed-upon guidelines for dealing with conflict.

Be aware that this group shares some of the load of conflict, which can be enervating. It offers care for hurting people who may hurt other people. It offers a chance for aggrieved parties to learn about communication and helps ensure that issues are dealt with objectively.

The SLA is not an advocate on behalf of the aggrieved parties or a mediator between the parties. The SLA team would not necessarily agree with the grievances of the complainant, but would commit itself to caring for those who hurt.

Creating Healthy and Responsible Church Bodies

We have been concerned with healthy, firm, and responsible ways for church bodies to respond to and deal with difficult behavior. None of these suggestions is easy. Before we move on to look at the responsibilities of church leaders, several cautions are in order.

First, church people may not be able to deal with conflict in healthy, responsible ways without considerable coaching and training, as well as observing good models of behavior. Many—possibly because of inexperience, a limited repertoire of skills, or inadequate ego strength—are unable to assert themselves. Whatever the reason, training and teaching are important. As well as learning basic fair fighting, people must learn to speak directly and to observe due process.

Second, it is tempting to focus on those who behave irresponsibly. While we attempt to hold folk accountable to responsible standards, guidelines, and processes, there is little more we can do. We cannot force people to be responsible, but we can help them meet the *consequences* of irresponsibility. Relying on a party to act responsibly gives that party excessive power to sabotage process!

We need to work with those who are the healthiest. When our church holds conflict-training events, someone always laments the fact that "those who need it most" (i.e., the dissatisfied, the disgruntled) are absent. The greatest problem in dealing with difficult behavior is that we spend too much energy focusing on the behavior and its practitioners, rather than encouraging health.

A purpose of this book is to help us understand difficult behavior so that it need not preoccupy us. Then we can deal with it directly and spend more time and energy on fostering healthy and responsible behavior in those most capable of it.

Finally, delegating responsibility often does not work. So delegate anxiety instead. Friedman sees delegating anxiety as a way of challenging:

> Challenge is the basic context of health and survival, of a person, of the family, of a religious organization, or even (in the course of evolution) of an entire species. When it comes to life and growth . . . one of the most fundamental advances in modern healing is that it is no longer limited to treating symptoms after a disease has struck, or even to eradicating the causative agents in the environment. Today it is common practice to inject the germs and viruses directly into an organism so as to stimulate and help it develop its own system of defense.[15]

The place where we challenge is not always where we see the greatest problem. There is a parallel in family and marital counseling. Therapists often work with only one partner, the one most motivated. Our first instinct might find that unfortunate: after all, the unmotivated one (who most "needs" it) is not coming. Friedman believes such situations are not hopeless: One can

> bring change to a relationship by "coaching" the motivated partner alone on how to get out of the "feedback" position and how to gain more self-differentiation. Indeed, progress can often be made faster this way. The more motivated and therefore more coachable family member is generally the one who calls, generally is the one who articulates the problem and always is the partner who is more capable of defining his or her positions in a nonblaming way. He or she also tends to be an overfunctioner rather than an underfunctioner, which works both ways. It is usually their overfunctioning which has put them in the more stressful position, thus supplying their greater need to upset the status quo. But it is also their quickness to initiate and willingness to function without waiting for the other which makes them the better candidate for coaching.[16]

Rather than blaming the unmotivated absentee, this approach distributes responsibility. Ironically, the nonattending partner often cannot change until the attending partner does. Any method that relies on the "weaker" one's presence or collaboration also sets that process up to easy sabotage by the one who is least motivated to take on the challenges and effort of change.

When a congregation was going through some struggles, it employed a conflict-management expert from the wider church to help it resolve the difficulties. Some of the most conflicted members, whose behavior might be labeled "difficult," refused to participate. "What can we achieve if 'they' don't come?" asked several church leaders. They did not realize that the church itself, especially the "stronger" members, could find healthier ways of responding to dissent and unhappiness.

An Unlikely Success Story?

In one congregation I served, a member had a host of emotional and relational problems. Although raised a Mennonite in a fairly sheltered community, his life had led to ostracism from that rural community for many years. Alcohol problems, failed marriages, business troubles, bankruptcy, and jail time were all subjects of much gossip "back home."

Slowly he became more and more involved with our urban congregation. It was a gradual process, as he found it difficult to trust any church people. And truth be told, we did not always know how to relate to him either. He was wrapped up in his own world, did not listen well, had difficulty relating to others, and often acted out in highly inappropriate ways.

Then the inevitable happened in our small, democratically oriented congregation: He was asked to lead worship. This was *not* my idea, but I was only the pastor and was not consulted. This was in the days long before I had ever heard of the concept of "nonanxious presence," and I expended considerable anxiety on what might happen.

As it turned out, the worship service was beautiful. This parishioner's opportunity for leadership revealed unexpected gifts. He skillfully guided our worship. He related well to the children. He was fully himself, and at the same time he drew our attention to God.

Two things in particular I remember about this experience. The first is that it had all kinds of unexpected pay-offs for this parishioner. Although he had already joined the church, he still felt like an outsider. The truth is that he *was* an outsider. He later told me that this was the day when for the first time he felt included and affirmed as a member. It was a turning point for him.

The second is his children's story, in which he talked about the familiar cliché, "If you have lemons, make lemonade." This advice had a special ring of truth coming from him, as his life had been full of lemons. But more than that, it also described our relationship to him. It would have been easy for us to write him off as a lemon. I almost did. But in the unexpected opportunity of including him in worship leadership, the challenge of his "lemony" quality became a gift of lemonade that quenched his thirst and ours.

CHAPTER 6

Trouble Is Our Business

Like many theological-minded types, I have a fondness for mysteries, all kinds. I particularly like the "hard-boiled" mysteries of such authors as Dashiell Hammett, Raymond Chandler, and Ross Macdonald. There, the lone private eye faces a *film noir* world. Admittedly the lone tough guy, even with a passion for truth and justice, is not exactly an ideal model for church leaders. Even so, I like Chandler's famous rendering of the challenge for literary detectives: It goes something like this: "Down these mean streets a [person] must go who is not . . . mean, who is neither tarnished nor afraid."[1]

I hate to be the bearer of bad news, but our best-intentioned efforts at dealing responsibly with difficult behavior may not work. In fact, they probably will not work! For to modify a famous Chandler title: Trouble is our business. If that seems a little too daunting or pessimistic, we can concede at least that *troubled* is our business!

Warning: Expect Sabotage!

A consultant working with a congregation on its conflict noted people's sincere efforts to function in a more healthy and responsible way. "Be careful," he warned. "When you start messing with the system, you don't know what backlash you might provoke!" Sensitive to family-systems dynamics, he was not discouraging the congregation from essential work. But he was matter-of-factly warning against naïveté about results: Systems or organizations, intentionally or not, do not always want to grow toward healthier functioning.

While we may grasp the benefits of dealing with difficult behavior in firm and responsible ways and while many leaders may also be so persuaded (at least in theory), do not expect such changed approaches to come easily. Systems tend toward "homeostasis"—that is, they like to return to things as they were before.

When people change their roles in a system, especially when they move toward more autonomy, independence, or differentiation, the rest of the group may try to persuade (or even force) the person to resume a previous role and stance. Edwin Friedman calls it "absolutely predictable" that other partners will try to sabotage or seduce one into behaving as one did previously![2] In fact, the more progress a leader makes toward healthy functioning, the stronger will be the reaction.

The Sabotage of Rumors

Any church leader will regularly encounter statements that begin like this: "Someone says . . . ," "Some are saying . . . ," or—more anxiety-provoking yet—"Many are saying . . ." Various reasons are given for anonymous information-sharing, but such reasons should be regarded with suspicion and vigorously challenged.

Churches are hotbeds of rumor, gossip, secrets, third-party complaints and murmuring. But these behaviors are not just difficult in themselves; they are often significant ways of *resisting* attempts at good health in our congregations. They enable and perpetuate difficult behavior.

Sometimes gossip and rumors are innocently called the "grapevine." Some believe that grapevines have a noble and essential ministry: ensuring that the whole community is kept informed of what is important. Positive potentials aside, systems theory takes a dim view of rumors, gossip, secrets, and murmuring.

Circulating information indirectly and secretly causes many problems. It easily tends to exaggeration and distortion. The person receiving the information does not understand the context of what is reported. Indirect anonymous communication can be a passive-aggressive cover. A simple problem between two people, communicated indirectly through rumors, may end up involving many more and spreading pain and anxiety further and further.

I experienced some problems when a member sent a long E-mail message about the difficulty of recruiting volunteers for a particular task and alluded to "one person who is very willing but [who is] being clandestinely shunned from leadership." I was alarmed on several counts. I wondered who the person in question was, what kinds of rumors were floating about, what kinds of conversations surfaced that charge, and (last but not least) whether the charge was true. When I asked the E-mailer directly what was intended, he told me the comment was tongue-in-cheek. My fears were alleviated and my anxieties allayed, once I could set aside the exaggeration and understand the context (which is often especially difficult in written communication).

Rumors follow a threefold pattern of distortion. First, "leveling": Basic details of context and explanation are dropped from the account, as they may soften the perspective. Second, "sharpening": Other details are exaggerated. Third, leveled and sharpened details are melded or "assimilated into the totally different context and mindset of the person who uses the rumor to get his own meaning and to accomplish his own purpose." Rumors, of course, can spread and grow: "a brush fire within the church system."[3] Rumors are especially enabled in a climate of simple poor communication or secrecy.

An elder asked why I charged $150 to marry couples. I was surprised: We neither charge fees for weddings nor expect an honorarium. Reflecting on the specificity of the number, I remembered encouraging couples to attend a premarital weekend elsewhere for which the fee was $150. The course was not required, and I offered financial assistance. Someone heard about this, but details were distorted as they made their way through the grapevine.

Secrets block communication. A major problem with secret, indirect information is not so much its *content* as the *effect* of this process. Friedman believes that the destructive consequences are predictable.[4] Secrets divide a community between those "in" on the secret and those "out" of it; this division then affects other issues in the group. As well as creating divisions, secrets also create pseudo-alliances. Secrets distort perceptions, confusing and misleading people. Most important, secrets keep anxiety high.

When people perpetuate secret information, they may claim to communicate someone else's agenda (what "someone else" said), but they communicate their own anxiety. Such behavior shows a problem in the system, possibly the absence of established grievance procedures. Leas notes that "distorted or interrupted communication," including anonymous communication, is the "problem most often identified in church conflicts." He contends that sharing information without the source is unethical.[5]

Peter Steinke notes that murmuring, grumbling, and secret complaining are roundly criticized in Scripture: Jude 16, Gal. 5:15, 1 Cor. 1:10-17, 2 Tim. 4:14, Exod. 16:7, Num. 14:27, Exod. 17:7, Num. 21:5, Luke 15:2, Acts 6:1, John 6:41, and John 6:61.[6] Rumors, gossip, secrets, third-party complaints, and murmuring are all related to the four viruses that Steinke believes

> can turn a congregation into a virtual "hot zone"—an anxiety pit. The viruses are *secrets* (gossiping, whispering), *accusations* (blaming, faultfinding), *lies* (deceiving), and *triangulation* (shifting burdens elsewhere). They are all expressions of . . . anxiety. The presence of secrets or triangles are not themselves the disease. Rather, secrets and triangles enable the disease process. The disease requires a combination of the secrecy and the host cells (people who permit secrets to exist).[7]

It is tempting to point fingers at people who gossip, spread rumors, anonymously accuse, and backbite. But such behavior exists *only* if the system itself permits and enables it.

One church I served actually institutionalized such behavior! A "voice from the pew" was appointed to sit on the administrative board as mouthpiece for any complaints brought to this person. The complaints were always handled anonymously. I noted a rise in anxiety whenever complaints were brought forward this way. It was difficult to weigh complaints: How serious is the person who is concerned? How many are concerned? How committed is the person to the church?

One anonymous complaint disclosed that someone felt that it was not hygienic for parishioners to break their own bread from the communion loaf. The board's first instinct was to make an immediate change in how communion was served. The validity of the concern was checked with and refuted by two nurses. Unfortunately, since the complaint was anonymous, we never knew whether the person indeed believed that we had legitimate reasons for continuing our particular communion practice. Such are the hazards of indirect and anonymous communication.

That complaint may have been truly held by an individual. Even more dangerous is the rush of anxious leaders to address *rumored* complaints. Anxious, unsure leaders may be deceived into thinking that problems are more serious than they are.

Responding to Rumors

Congregations and leaders can responsibly deal with the sabotage of rumors, gossip, secrets, third-party complaints, and murmuring. Since the complicity of the "host" church enables such unhealthy and anxious behaviors, the choice must be made by the church itself to change its responses to such behaviors.

We need to remember that we cannot change the behavior of others or force them to be responsible. Gossipmongers, backbiters, and complainers might make a nice target for our own gossiping, backbiting, and complaining, but that is no help. Congregations and their leaders are called to healthier functioning.

There are two primary principles for disabling rumors, gossip, secrets, and third-party complaints. First, since secrecy is a serious part of the problem, churches and leaders should not keep secrets *about* secrets. Exposing secrecy can feel frightening, especially in a system that is used to secrets (and when the group's norms or family rules encourage secrecy). I remember my own anxiety and uneasiness in first studying my family of origin, when I was assigned to identify and name unspoken family rules and secrets. But liberation is possible in this process: When secrets are revealed, anxiety usually decreases.

Refusing to keep secrets about secrets means *naming* and *addressing* unhealthy behavior. Some believe that gossip, rumors, or anonymous complaints will "just go away" if ignored. But ignoring such behavior perpetuates it. Admitting, exposing, and naming such difficult behaviors is the first step in overcoming them. We "host" them by keeping secret about them.

The second principle is this: Viruses cannot be spread if we do not spread them. We disable rumors, gossip, secrets, third-party complaints, and murmuring by refusing to pass them on or perpetuate them. "For lack of wood the fire goes out, and where there is no whisperer, quarreling ceases" (Prov. 26:20). (Such ancient passages remind us how long-standing and ingrained our patterns and systems of conflict are!)

Churches can be debilitated by gossip and accusations. When people make accusations without addressing either the proper authorities or the offenders, they hurt the community. If you hear a rumor about someone, check with him or her directly about what you have heard. Also respond to rumors at their source. If leaders believe gossip is happening, they should gather some information: Find out *who* is gossiping, have evidence of the gossip, and speak to the offender directly.

Rumors can be undermined by providing prompt and accurate information about decisions and process. When a congregation experienced a high degree of conflict, the board decided to write up a regular newsletter about decisions and church events. This simple act was one of the most popular moves the board ever made. Correct information is especially important when rumors are apt to spread or are already spreading.

Boards should not act on anonymous charges or complaints. If there is a "voice from the pew," let concerns be brought with a name attached. Otherwise we encourage immature, irresponsible, and unaccountable power. Do not give power without responsibility. The board should act only on information from a known source. Anonymous criticism should be disregarded.

If a person claims to speak on behalf of others, insist that names be cited. Leaders and other church folk are often triangulated when people confidentially complain to them about a third party. If that happens, the best policy is to be direct here as well. Speed Leas, in his lectures, has recommended a series of questions:

- "Have you spoken to so-and-so?" Encourage that person to discuss his or her concerns with the other party. One might coach a person in how to do this.
- Failing that, you might ask, "May I go with you?" Offer to *accompany* the person so that he or she can state the case directly to the other. Accompaniment should be neutral: You go *not* to be on any "side" but to help both parties speak and be heard.
- The next question might be surprising: "May I tell so-and-so your concern?" This ploy breaks the secrecy and anonymity of the triangle. In a lecture, Leas wryly noted that such approaches and questions communicate an important message: "I'm no fun to complain to."

Leas also addresses situations in which someone offers information with this condition: "Will you keep this confidential if I tell you?" Leas recommends a conditional response: "It depends on what the information is."

While firm behavior is healthier for all involved, it will not always meet with universal approval. Some people simply do not have the ego strength to learn firm and direct address. Nevertheless, responsible leaders need to behave this way. While the effects on others cannot be guaranteed, persistence is essential.

Direct approaches to indirect behavior will be difficult to learn for those more practiced in indirect ways. Most will have to practice these styles. These standards, however, are worth setting, declaring, and upholding; they are a mark of emotional health. Steinke argues that such direct approaches are rooted in biblical models.

> Secret behavior is . . . utterly neglectful of the evangelical counsel "to speak the truth in love." In the New Testament three prominent situations address anxious reactivity in the Christian community: the Matthean sayings (Matthew 5:21-24; 7:3; 18:15-22); the Council of Jerusalem (Acts 15); and the chaos at Corinth (1 Corinthians 1:12; 3:4). Each situation calls for personalizing the conflict, face-to-face meetings, and sunlight for disinfecting the disease.[8]

The Contemporary Relevance of Matthew 18

> If another member of the church sins against you, go and point out the fault when the two of you are alone. If the member listens to you, you have regained that one. But if you are not listened to, take one or two others along with you, so that every word may be confirmed by the evidence of two or three witnesses. If the member refuses to listen to them, tell it to the church; and if the offender refuses to listen even to the church, let such a one be to you as a Gentile and a tax collector (Matt. 18:15-18).

From their movement's beginnings, Anabaptists regarded Matt. 18:15-20, "the Rule of Christ," as especially important in church life. For some, it assured that the church was "pure" and "visible" (as opposed to the notion that the true church was an invisible part of the visible church).

I have heard many stories about church discipline in the past but have not seen any formal church discipline in my years as a pastor. Rueful regrets over previous harsh discipline and a modern pluralist sensibility have eroded the possibility of administering Matt. 18. As Mennonite theologian and ethicist John Howard Yoder observed: "We are afraid in our modern polite pluralism to tell anyone that our communion with them has limits."[9]

Yet the passage from Matt. 18 occupies an especially important place in Scripture.

It is the only place we find the word "church" reported as being used by Jesus himself. Its weight is accented by the account of Paul's asking the Christians in Corinth to use this procedure instead of going to the Gentile courts (1 Corinthians 6:1-8), and by the explicit command closing the letter of James (5:19-20).[10]

Matt. 18 still has useful principles to apply to conflictual and difficult behavioral situations today. Several points are worth noting.

The text suggests frequent attempts to make the relationship work. Leas says that many rush to premature resolution, closure, or even expulsion rather than persist at the hard work of resolution. This conclusion was also confirmed by Menno Epp's study of forced terminations: Little effort was made to restore relationships.[11]

Matt. 18:15-17 still applies to various church scenarios. It fits into the norms and fair-fighting rules that we recommended earlier. The process involves three stages.

- First, if one is offended, go first to the person who caused the offense and speak to him or her *directly*.
- Second, if that fails, bring others along to help with the discussion and serve as witnesses (not as allies or supporters).
- And, finally, "If the member refuses to listen to them, tell it to the church; and if the offender refuses to listen even to the church, let such a one be to you as a Gentile and a tax collector" (Matt. 18:17).

With each step, the circle of people included in the process grows: from private confrontation, to confrontation with witnesses, to involvement of the congregation as a whole. Confidentiality is guarded as long as possible.

A possible problem: Matt. 18 seems to make clear who is right and who is wrong. That certainly is often not the case in conflicts. In fact, we do well to be especially cautious when we are convinced that we are in the right: It is too tempting to enter a conflict with a crusading mentality. Thus we enter confrontations gently and humbly.

Each step of Matt. 18 is an opportunity and an attempt to get people to hear each other better and to recognize each other's concerns. As Yoder points out, Matt. 18 is not recommended as guarantecing the church's purity or reputation, exemplifying God's righteousness, making church membership demanding, or guarding against the erosion of values. The real purpose is reconciliation; i.e., the restoration of relationships. The priority of restoration and reconciliation is the reason for so many attempts. This procedure has been used as a tool for punishing people, but its evident hope is restoration and reconciliation.[12]

Yoder sees several possible errors when applying Matt. 18[13]—first, focusing on punishment rather than reconciliation; second, concentrating on the offense rather than the person; third, worrying more about rules and standards than about the person.

Treating the unreconciled sibling "as a Gentile and a tax collector" is curious. Some take this passage to mean rejection and cut-off. But Jesus was often criticized for associating with Gentiles and tax collectors. So Matt. 18 in fact suggests openness to seeing the unreconciled one return and reconcile.

The Rule of Christ is matter-of-fact about how the best-intentioned efforts do not always work. Sometimes people need to release each other. Leas compares this point to Jesus' words about shaking the dust from one's feet. "It is a clear message: when you are not accepted, go elsewhere; do not endlessly strive to get through to the other."[14] (Some suggest that "shaking the dust" off our feet should be a sacrament!) But releasing or giving up happens only after many attempts. It is not the prematurely precipitous "flight" or expulsion that is often the first unhealthy reaction to problems or conflicts.

While it is a danger to "rush to judgment" and expel, my experience is the opposite. I usually see people unwilling to open up sensitive subjects, let alone confront one another over problems and violations of trust. In the impulse to togetherness (sometimes called "the urge to merge"), people are most frightened that someone might leave. When people left our congregations, the sorrow was great. (Ironically, people often leave because hurtful things were *ignored*.) This is particularly so in small, "single-cell" churches where each person's individuality makes up such a large part of the church's identity.

Here, we must remember two things. First, we need to know when to let others go or even to encourage them to move on. At times we cannot offer what they need. At times they cannot be happy or content in our churches because their ideas and vision are so different from the group's.

As noted earlier, there are times when it is appropriate to ask others to leave.

Second, people sometimes choose to leave or withdraw. At times, the threat of withdrawal can be a goad to persuade the congregation to do one's will. This ploy is especially effective in groups that highly value togetherness. In my present congregation, deep wounds and griefs persist over people who left because their theological vision did not match that of our congregation (or even of our denomination).

When someone leaves, debrief with them and find out the reasons. Such "exit interviews" might be an occasion for reconciliation and perhaps even restoration. If closure and parting can be arranged, that too is helpful. Ironically, although our congregation hates to see people go, members almost never ask former parishioners *why* they left!

Sometimes it is best for the Body of Christ that someone does leave. When an individual's stance is radically different from the group's, then perhaps the individual's

> stewardship and outlook can effectively be used by God in another place and perhaps more effectively be channeled by another congregation. Pastor and caring leaders sometimes need to bless this departure as inspired by God.[15]

It is not necessarily a loss to the Body of Christ when a person leaves for another congregation. We need a broader sense of God's working through the various gifts and callings of different congregations, denominations, and traditions. Too often we think that we must have all our specific ideas precisely correct, and hence (by implication) everyone else must be wrong. We need to have a broader idea of church: Although we cannot necessarily agree with one another and although we do not understand one another, yet we can trust that God is at work in one another.

This belief is illustrated in Acts 15:35-40. Paul and Barnabas, coworkers and successful missionaries, veterans of a few church conflicts themselves, have a falling out. This story could be seen as embarrassing. They have just successfully come through the major conflict earlier in Acts 15, helping the church find a meaningful compromise on the inclusion of Gentile believers.

As they are about to embark on another missionary tour, Barnabas wants to take young John Mark. But Paul does not trust this fellow who abandoned them earlier. Barnabas—mediator, encourager, and upholder of underdogs—wants to give John Mark another chance. "The disagreement became so sharp that they parted company; Barnabas took Mark with him and sailed away to Cyprus" (Acts 15:39-40). Paul and Silas went another direction.

The text does not tell us who, if either, was correct. Both men recognized that they could not work together. In the interest of the church, they parted. Both did good works. Both are recognized as saints in church tradition. The conflict and split were sad, to be sure. Ironically, now there were *two* missions rather than one. And John Mark, the young man in question, may well have been the person who eventually penned the Gospel of Mark.

Paul and Barnabas fought but also made a mature decision to go separate ways. They did not excommunicate each other. (Some, overfond of the Rule of Christ, have done much excommunicating over the centuries!) But for the good and priority of the Gospel, Paul and Barnabas knew they needed to part.

Sometimes believers have to say: "I do not agree with you. I disagree with you sharply. I do not know how to agree with you. But for the good of the Gospel, the well-being of the church, why do you not go your way and I go mine, and may God go with us both, bless us both, and perhaps someday we can reconnect in a healthier way."

Such partings may hurt, feel sad, and seem tragic. But sometimes that is the only way for the necessary work of the church to proceed.

CHAPTER 7

Stray Dogs and Whistlers' Conventions

The members of a recently established urban church were exhausted. This congregation, composed of young and middle-aged adults, was not many years old but faced a years-long process of dealing with a pastor's sexual boundary-crossing.

One day, in great frustration, a young adult church leader complained: "You know, this isn't fair. We don't have any older people here to make the decisions and take the responsibility! Then at least we could blame them!" Others at the meeting were surprised by his sentiment, but it was devastatingly honest.

It also reminds us that congregations are simply not always capable of carrying out the responsible leadership we have been examining and proposing. This means that church leaders must take on greater responsibility.

I like a legend, which I have heard in more than one version, of a great spiritual teacher whose goal, when she was young, was to change the world. At middle age, she narrowed her ambition to changing her family and community. Finally, in her mature years, she realized that it was only she herself she could change. Ironically, as she changed, all around her were affected as well.

I have heard that "pastoring is like being a stray dog at a whistlers' convention." But leadership means that we will not live that way, responding to every whistle we hear (whether or not it is meant for us). Leadership requires setting directions for ourselves.

The Crucial Role of the Pastor as Leader

One of the most difficult lessons for me as a pastor was to learn that I am not "just one of the gang." Christians casually bat around the "priesthood of all believers," assuming it means that everyone is called to church leadership. When I first became a pastor, I never wore a tie: I wanted to be as informal as everyone else in that congregation, "one of the gang." I wanted to be low-key and not "on a pedestal." Like most ministers in my denomination, I never use a title (such as "Reverend"), except when doing advocacy on behalf of someone else.

While still not interested in pedestals, I gradually learned that pastors are never "just one of the gang." When I was called to my present assignment, my wife and I looked at many homes before moving. We later discovered that we twice looked at homes directly adjacent to the homes of church members. When we reported this to the respective members, both responded the same way: "I wonder what it would be like to live beside the pastor." At the time, the question seemed odd—"What's the issue?"— but I understand it better now: My role does set me apart.

I learned the same lesson more painfully after leaving a church as a consequence of a deep conflict. Several people said they were pleased that "no members" left as a result of the conflict. My wife and I were baffled and hurt by such remarks. For surely we were members, and we were leaving. But that telling comment taught us that, although we may not be on a pedestal, we are in a different category.

On a broader scale, church structures have learned the same thing. Denominations, schools, and congregations have been rocked by revelations of clergy sexual abuse and the crossing of sexual boundaries. Such abuse is a violation of trust, not just another case of sexual infidelity but a misuse of power. We appropriately call church leaders to higher standards than those we expect of members in the pew. While such realities may be hard to swallow for those who pretend that all in the church have the same calling, systems theorists show us that the position and role of congregational leaders have important implications.

Thus, while it is important to consider healthy congregational responses to difficult behavior, as we have, it is vital to consider the responsibilities of church leaders. The truth is that many congregations either do not know how to respond to destructive behavior responsibly or are incapable of doing so. Whether we like it or not, the implication is clear: Leaders are on the front line, and our responses are crucial.

Hugh Halverstadt makes a similar point when he discusses roles in conflicts. In his terminology, "parties" in conflicts represent wider interests than just their own, whether those interests are official structures, a particular clique, a specific theological orientation, or a special-interest group. Parties never act only as individuals but

> are parties to virtually every major church fight in the parish they serve. . . . Pastors have little choice over whether they will be parties to a conflictive situation.[1]

Family-systems theory says that the pastor as leader is crucial. The pastor is not separate from the congregation: Rather the pastor plays a unique role in the system. This role gives certain responsibilities. Peter Steinke says pastoral leaders can be either the "ruin" or the "salvation" of a church.[2] Such a choice can sound intimidating. While pastors cannot choose *whether* to be involved, they can choose *how* to be involved. The issue, then, comes down to choices and decisions about how to respond appropriately to challenges.

This decision can feel onerous. Many prefer to put responsibility for difficult behavior elsewhere. But to do so is to shirk our responsibility as leaders. Oddly enough, this style can be the less stressful choice. It involves owning what is our responsibility and delegating responsibility. Edwin Friedman believes that this approach decreases stress and actually leads to less acting out or burnout on the part of clergy.[3]

Differentiated Leadership

Differentiation is a key notion. It is the ability to be a "self" or an "I" in the face of pressure by others or systems to be part of, or blend into, the "we." To be differentiated is to know and act on one's own mind, especially when our position is different from the group's. It means to know one's opinion, stand, or stance without imposing expectations or demands on others. It is the ability to state clearly and calmly our position without suggesting (with "must," "should," or "ought" language) that others need to have the same position.

Here is a key to why responsible leadership is less onerous than other forms of leadership. Differentiated leaders realize that their primary and ultimate responsibility is taking charge of self and not changing, motivating, or shifting others. As the truism goes, "We cannot change others, only ourselves." This is far less debilitating and draining than focusing all one's energies on getting others to do things right; one focuses on oneself, rather than on everyone else in the system.

Differentiation happens first in our family of origin. In Luke's account of Jesus in the temple (Luke 2:41-52) Jesus begins the work of differentiation from his parents. Contrary to their expectations, this 12-year-old remains behind in the temple after the Passover feast. After three days, the parents discover him there, competently relating to the teachers. They respond anxiously: "Child, why have you treated us like this? Look, your father and I have been searching for you in great anxiety" (2:48). Jesus calmly replies: "Did you not know that I must be in my Father's house?" (2:49).

The story about Jesus is significant in another way. Adolescence is a time when children feel the pull toward differentiation. Those so-called "difficult teenage years" are the adolescent's move toward adulthood and a measure of autonomy. The less differentiated the parents are, the more difficult it will be for them to deal with the teenager's quest for differentiation.

The challenge and responsibility of differentiation begin at home. Leaders who are not differentiated in their family of origin will not function well in the church family. Family-of-origin work is crucial to good leadership. Pastors deal with three families: families *in* the congregation, the congregation as family, and their own family; "unresolved issues in any one of them can produce symptoms in the others, and increased understanding of any one creates more effective functioning in all three."[4]

I experienced this truth when my father died. I had not done family-of-origin work, and within a year I was embroiled in a major conflict with a church patriarch! Unresolved family-of-origin issues inevitably affect our performance in marriage or in the parish.

There is a flip side to the interrelationship between parish and family of origin. The way parishioners relate to leaders (especially in projection and transference) has a lot to do with their differentiation (or lack thereof) in their own family.

This connection has two implications. One, when we understand people's varying levels of differentiation, we are less apt to overreact anxiously when we see them "misbehave"; i.e., act undifferentiated. This insight helps us to deal more realistically with them. Two, it challenges us both to serve as models of differentiation and to coach church members to achieve differentiation and to work through their family-of-origin issues.

Edwin Friedman has a simple test to determine congregants' levels of differentiation.

> All we have to do is give a talk in which we carefully differenti-
> ate ourselves—define clearly what we believe and where we stand
> on issues, in a way that is totally devoid of "shoulds" and "musts."
> The response of the congregational family . . . will always range
> along the following spectrum. Those who function emotionally to-
> ward the "better differentiated" end will respond *by defining them-
> selves*: "Father, I agree"; "I disagree"; "I believe"; etc. or, "Ms.
> Jones, I like what you said, though I am not sure I can agree with
> you on. . . ." Those at the "less well-differentiated" end will re-
> spond not by defining themselves but by continuing *to define their
> clergyman or clergywoman*: "Father, how can you say that when
> . . ."; "Ms. Smith, how do you reconcile this with what you said
> the other day when you . . . "; "Rabbi, sometimes I wonder if you
> are even Jewish."[5]

It is important to know people's level of differentiation because it helps us anticipate how they will deal with problems or crises, both at home and in the church.

Leadership through differentiation is not always effective, but it does have advantages.

> It fosters independence without encouraging polarization and it
> allows interdependence without promoting cults. It seeks to pro-
> mote togetherness but not at the cost of progress. It normalizes
> transition, and it is less susceptible to cut-offs. Most of all, . . . it
> reverses the pull and drain of dependents who normally gain power
> from the expectation . . . that their demand to be included at their
> price and pace will always be satisfied. It also has advantages for
> the leader. . . . It makes his or her job less complex, yet gives
> more leverage. . . . It reduces enervating conflicts of wills (and
> triangles). . . . Finally, because the approach is less load-bearing
> and more self-expressive, it minimizes the influence of the fac-
> tors that contribute to burnout.[6]

In spirituality, differentiation is closely connected to *solitude*, the alone place where we encounter the truth about ourselves by being confronted with the truth and reality of God. Solitude offers a possibility of conversion, change, transformation, growth, and rebirth. As an introvert, I can easily mistake such emphasis on solitude as a welcome excuse for being solitary. But biblical faith does not allow me to rest easy in my proclivity to privacy.

There are many conversion-in- or call-in-solitude stories in the Bible: the encounter of Moses with God in the burning bush (Exod. 3), the Transfiguration witnessed by Peter, James, and John (Mark 9:2-13), the Pentecost story when the believers were still separated and fearful (Acts 2), Paul's encounter with the risen Christ on the Damascus road (Acts 9).

Each of these stories has a quality of apartness, separateness, or solitude. The called or converted are away from the crowd and their normal routine when something new is revealed. Their solitude was not a cozy, comfortable retreat or escape, but the solitude of dislocation, pain, and exile. There they encountered questions, challenge, and uncertainty.

In each circumstance, the believer was not invited to stay in a private, protected place. Rather the experience was intended to lead *back* to engagement with wider reality. Moses was invited to respond to God's concerns: "I have observed the misery of my people who are in Egypt. I have heard their cry on account of their taskmasters. Indeed, I know their sufferings" (Exod. 3:7). Immediately after the Transfiguration, in all three synoptic gospels, the disciples encounter a demoniac (Mark 9:14-29; Matt. 17:14-21; Luke 9:37-43). The disciples in the upper room were not baptized in the Spirit for spiritual titillation but so that the Good News could be spread further. Paul encountered Jesus in solitude and was called to a daring and costly ministry.

A major achievement of differentiation is realizing that one's own happiness or contentment resides in oneself and not in the other. Years ago, the first time I read Friedman, I recognized a cycle in my family relationships. A family member would be mildly depressed or "down." I would strive mightily to cheer him or her up. I pinned *my* ability for contentment on their demeanor. (As a pastor, I often function as a "rescuer.") If my efforts failed, I would become angry at the other. Friedman helped me realize that each person is responsible for his or her own happiness. Trying to make the other happy is futile. Ironically, once I stopped anxiously pressuring others to be happy and stopped worrying about whether they were content, they often became more content. Here is where systemic change often begins in families and churches. Differentiation can decrease conflict when one party stops pressuring the other.

Differentiation and Staying in Touch

Differentiation does not mean being autonomous, cut off, separate, or independent. The leader needs to be oneself and remain part of the system. This is not necessarily easy. The trick is to be connected with people but not to condition one's emotions on them.

One temptation for the leader is to lose touch, cut off, or withdraw. But cutting off is not differentiation. Cutting oneself off from others does not show a lack of emotion but *too much* emotion and an inability to cope with that intensity of emotion.

I have seen many cut-offs on both sides of my own family: in each instance cut-offs were caused not by a *lack* of feeling but by a *surplus* of emotions that one or both parties did not know how to handle. After my grandfather emigrated, he never communicated again with his brother who remained behind in the Netherlands. Their facial and vocal resemblance was uncanny. They had much in common, but 40 years passed with no communication between them. No one knows what the issues were. Systems thinking tells me not that the two men were uncaring and unfeeling, but rather that they did not know how to handle intense feelings.

If we do not guard against withdrawal or cut-offs on the basis of family-systems wisdom, then perhaps we can do so because of hard practical experience. In his study of the forced exits of pastors, Menno Epp notes that pastors often withdraw or cut off in the face of criticism, dissent, dissatisfaction, or unhappiness. While understandable, such withdrawal often backfires by making things worse; the withdrawal often "communicated what pastors care not to be accused of, namely, lack of caring, abandonment and coldness."[7] Withdrawal is ill-advised and ineffective. Crises that tempt us to cut off may actually be an opportunity for a new phase of ministry.

Differentiation means that the leader finds healthy ways of staying in touch and connected with the congregation.

Differentiation and Taking Nonreactive Stands

Leaders may be tempted to stay "in touch" without being differentiated. This fits our stereotype of "wishy-washy" politicians who move "whichever way the wind blows." They do not declare themselves or their positions for fear that someone might disagree and hence not vote for them. But it is unhealthy to base too many decisions on the wish to avoid upsetting others.

Friedman says another element of differentiation is the ability to take clearly articulated and nonreactive positions. He explains how this skill works in family therapy when the therapist helps people take "I" positions.

> An "I" position . . . defines self; it is saying, "I like, "I don't like," "I believe," "I don't agree," "I am going to do this," "I am not going to do that," etc. It is mutually exclusive of "you," "us," and "we" positions such as, "You always—," or "We should—," which are cohortative, or coercive, blaming.[8]

The challenge is to take an I-stand and stay in touch. Too often I-stands ("Here I stand!") are all-or-nothing ways of drawing a line, declaring war, issuing a threat or ultimatum, all of which make it more difficult to connect. One reason adults regard adolescence as "difficult teen years" is that teenagers often are not skilled at declaring and defining themselves and keeping healthy contact. Parents, of course, often have the same problem!

A leader's declaring nonreactive "I-stands" can liberate healthy, self-differentiated people in the congregation. Defining ourselves is one of the main contributions we make to parishioners. The results may be surprising. When the leader tries to change his or her followers, then the followers are "in charge" and can sabotage the leader. The followers then are in control. But this outcome is reversed when a leader exercises leadership.

Of course, it is not enough for a leader to declare opinions or stands. The leader must be prepared to follow through with them.

Dealing with Sabotage

Lest we become naïvely optimistic about the guaranteed or unqualified benefits of differentiation, Friedman notes another element of differentiation: being able to deal with sabotage. The better we are at acting in a well-differentiated fashion, the more likely we are to encounter resistance and even sabotage.

Once again, we can look at the parallel situations of growth and change in families. In marriage, when one partner differentiates, the other often responds with seduction or sabotage. This urge to stay the same (or homeostasis) is inherent in all systems. Intriguingly, *only now* can true change happen.

Therapists might coach the differentiating partner ahead of time on what kinds of reactions the other partner might indulge in to sabotage growth: physical abuse, substance abuse, depression, an extramarital affair, excessive criticism, temper tantrums, threats or ultimatums, suicide attempts. With preparation, one need not be thrown by sabotage. Friedman suggests that the partner being counseled can tell the other partner which anxious responses are anticipated and encourage the other to take responsibility for them.

> It can be done straightforwardly, such as, "I must tell you that I expect you will probably get sick (become depressed, be critical), but I will not cater to you this time," or more playfully, "Well, if you are so upset, why don't you have an affair (get drunk, pick on the kids). That usually makes you feel better." Of course, the straightforward approach may run more risk of being a dare, while the mischievous response usually challenges the other to keep self-control.[9]

Leaders too consider the possibility that their differentiation may lead to sabotage. One can try to anticipate the sabotage and prepare accordingly. While sabotage may feel off-putting and distancing, the behavior actually is intended to bring us back into a togetherness mode: The separation of differentiation is too uncomfortable for the system.

The stronger the reaction, the less differentiation the reactor has and the more he or she will react against the progress and growing health of his or her leader. This tendency is closely related to the level of differentiation in families.

Ironically, our best behavior may bring out the worst behavior in others. Leaders must not be surprised, hurt, or offended by this reaction. Leaders are called to responsibility and growth, and this role can be lonely. Leadership includes the willingness to be misunderstood. Our differentiation is not assured until we can respond to sabotage in a healthy way without retribution, rigidity or dogmatism, cut-off or withdrawal.

Differentiation is not a way to persuade people to join you but a way to encourage them to be differentiated. Pastoral counselor Ronald Richardson cites biblical examples. Jesus predicted he would be killed in Jerusalem and later that the disciples would abandon him. They disagreed, but Jesus proceeded without "their cooperation or agreement or even their understanding. . . ." Paul told Jerusalem church leaders that the Gospel was also meant for Gentiles, who did not need to be circumcised. He proceeded "mostly without full understanding or support of the church's leaders." Proceeding despite misunderstanding and lack of support, Jesus and Paul also maintained connections, staying in touch.

> Neither Jesus nor Paul cut off from those people who disagreed with them. The disciples and the church leaders distanced themselves from Jesus and Paul, but Jesus and Paul did not let themselves be overcome with feelings of abandonment . . . or become reactive to the reactivity of the others. They maintained their side of the connection and got on with their understanding of their mission. Eventually the church joined them at a new level of functioning.[10]

A Nonanxious Presence

During a meeting with a mentor/supervisor I received an urgent message that a beloved parishioner (who had recently been maimed in a serious accident) had been diagnosed with cancer. I was understandably shaken by the news. My mentor and I decided to cut short our meeting so that I could immediately go to the parishioner. Before I left, my mentor said to me in passing: "Remember: You bear the presence of Christ."

As I drove to the hospital, I repeated these wise words to myself and pondered them. They seemed obvious, but I needed to hear them at that moment. By the time I reached the parishioner I had calmed down sufficiently to be a listening, caring minister, rather than someone who was panicked and needy because of my own reactions. My supervisor had steered me toward being nonanxious (or at least *less* anxious!).

We all face stress. Comedian and actor Lily Tomlin is reported to have said: "Reality is the leading cause of stress among those in touch with it." Stress has positive potential: It can be an invitation to understanding or appropriate response. Anxiety, often our response to stress, also has positive potentials. It is helpful when it warns us about actual dangers. It is useful when it helps us prepare for challenges ahead—for example, in studying for a test. It can provide energy and motivation for creativity and change. The problem with anxiety comes when it affects (and often overwhelms) our thinking. Rather than learning from it as we learn from an alarm, we allow it to set our agenda.

Our brain has three layers. The brainstem is the most elementary, sometimes called "reptilian." It controls *automatic* processes, including breathing and blood circulation. The next layer is the limbic system (or "mammalian" brain), which controls emotional responses. When we respond automatically in the face of danger or threat, these parts of the brain are activated. The largest part of our brain, the cerebral hemispheres, controls conscious, rational thought. Both the brainstem and the limbic system are instinctual, automatic, and reactive. Cerebral hemispheres, however, are thoughtful, inventive, and responsive.

When overwhelmed by anxiety, we revert to automatic processes of the lower brain. We react automatically, even when that does not serve us well. Lower spheres also act more quickly than the higher level. When we feel fear or some other pressing emotion, the brain "triggers the secretion of the body's fight-or-flight hormones, mobilizes the centers for movement and activates the cardiovascular system, the muscles, and the gut."[11] These physical responses can have behavioral consequences: Impulsivity overwhelms intention, instinct overrules imagination, reflexes rule out reflection, defensiveness dominates, and options appear limited. Herein lies the problem: "In periods of intense anxiety, what is most needed is what is most unavailable—the capacity to be imaginative."[12]

During times of high anxiety, emotions and automatic instinctual responses can take over. Daniel Goleman calls these takeovers "emotional hijackings" or being "engulfed." Steinke calls them "gusts of anxiety." At such times we are less imaginative, and our ability to learn is diminished.[13] "Anxious" comes from the Latin *angustia*, which means *narrowness*. Anxiety narrows and constricts our perceptions, responses, and abilities.

At this level, our brain acts defensively with either a fight, flight, or freeze reaction.[14]

This process has application to dealing with conflict or difficult behavior.

> Whenever people feel threatened or under attack . . . the emotional system begins to get out of control. The threat may not even appear particularly dangerous. It could just be a feeling people have when they are not getting what they wanted or expected from others, their life, or the church. The attack or threat does not have to be intentional. . . . The sense of being under attack often has to do with people's perceptions, which are based on their life experience over many years. They tend to interpret present-day experiences in terms of those historical experiences. Because these historical experiences (particularly those in our family of origin) are so powerful for all of us, they tend to control our current functioning.[15]

Anxiety adversely affects a community's health. It "magnifies differences" and decreases "capacity to tolerate or manage differences." Clarity and objectivity diminish.[16]

We saw earlier that Steinke divides anxiety into situational/acute and chronic/habitual. Situational/acute is time-limited, confined to particular situations. This anxiety passes when the crisis is over. Chronic/habitual anxiety is ongoing; it does not end.

> Some church families, unfortunately, are chronically anxious. Chronically anxious church families may have small groups splinter off periodically. Or the family stays intact but is submissive to a small but manipulative power group. In other chronically anxious church families, leadership changes rapidly, or change is always stalled and change agents are punished.[17]

Anxiety can be contagious. In relationships it maintains and reinforces itself; anxiety produces reactions (inflexibility, polarization) that create more anxiety.

In meetings of ministers, I often hear Steinke's phrase "nonanxious presence," which many first learned from Friedman. To be nonanxious is the capacity to respond appropriately and not to react. The ability to be nonanxious, calm, unpanicked, and nonreactive in the face of various stressors is helpful for two reasons: Leaders are more clearheaded and skillful, and a nonanxious presence calms the entire system. Being nonanxious helps everyone think more clearly, reasonably, carefully, imaginatively, creatively, and freely.

Friedman explains that clergy play a major role in how anxiety is dealt with in the congregation. We are like transformers in electrical circuits.

> To the extent we are anxious ourselves, . . . it becomes potentiated and feeds back into the congregational family at a higher voltage. But to the extent we can recognize and contain our own anxiety, then we function as step-down transformers, or . . . circuit breakers. In that case, our presence, far from escalating emotional potential, actually serves to diminish its "zapping" effect.[18]

We have practical, self-interested motives for heeding the recommendation to be nonanxious.

> Hostile congregational environments never victimize automatically. The response of clergy to their environment is almost always the main factor that determines how harmful it will be.[19]

Speed Leas notes another practical reason to be a nonanxious presence: A calm atmosphere is crucial for healthy work on conflict. First, fear and anxiety harm clear and rational thinking and thus impede the ability to tackle difficult situations. Second, the leader often can address the causes of the fear that underlie conflict, such as fear of being rejected, disliked, criticized, etc. A major leadership task in conflictual situations is to ease fears and anxieties. Our words and demeanor play a large role. *"Nothing works better in dealing with fear than direct, calm assurance on the part of the leader that the idea of disaster you are now anticipating is not likely to come to fruition."*[20] Leas tells a story to illustrate a nonanxious presence:

> I recall an experience I had on a jet that lost its hydraulic system in the air, leaving it without brakes, without the mechanism to automatically lower the landing gear, and without the use of the regular controls for steering the plane. The pilot described the situation, told us what he was going to do, and then related his training to

deal with such situations and implied that though this was unusual everything could be handled rather easily and simply. Instead of increasing our fear all the more, he did quite the opposite by arousing our confidence in his training, ability, and experience to deal with just such a situation as we were now experiencing.

A potential high-anxiety situation was defused. Leas saw the following practical elements as helpful:

- Statements of assurance that this could be handled
- A calm and relaxed demeanor and voice
- A clear description of what was happening and what it meant
- An understandable plan which was being put into effect to deal with the situation.

Note that the pilot did not command "Don't panic," "Relax," or "Don't be afraid." Rather his calm helped others remain calm too. Leaders help others manage anxiety first by managing their own anxiety. Then they can maintain meaningful contact with others.

The concept of the "nonanxious presence" is always affirmed when I hear it discussed by pastors. But sooner or later, someone asks, "Yes, but *how* do I do this?" Church consultant John A. Coil believes that three elements are important for becoming nonanxious in an anxious system.[21]

- First, understand how the system in which we work functions. It is best to do this work in consultation with others.
- Second, the leader must examine and understand his or her own anxiety in this situation. This step may require some reflection on similar anxieties in one's life; it can be done through counseling, journaling, spiritual direction, or consultation.
- Finally, when the first two steps are done well, the leader is able to be well-differentiated yet stay connected.

In discussing differentiation, Richardson also advocates important steps.[22]

1. Leaders need to be aware of their reactivity and its effect in the emotional system. As already suggested, there are many means to greater self-awareness. We must particularly ask ourselves why certain people or certain behaviors "push our buttons."

For example, I react strongly to people who act dogmatically and judgmentally. It was a long time before I noticed that this behavior that bothers me does not necessarily upset all others. In family-of-origin work, I realized that my reaction has much to do with my relationship to my father, a man of strong opinions and quick judgments. Now when I find myself reacting against particular people or behaviors, I caution myself to pull back and examine the situation more closely and carefully.

2. Leaders learn how to reduce anxiety in difficult situations. Employ a variety of stress-reducing strategies: leave a meeting briefly, take a break, breathe slowly and deeply, pray. Goleman considers the ability to control impulses a major part of emotional intelligence.[23]

3. Leaders need to separate intellect and emotion. Emotions should not be mistaken for facts. Emotions are important, but decisions need to be based ultimately on intellect. Goleman's book *Emotional Intelligence,* by the way, is an eloquent description of and argument for *intelligent* emotions.

4. Finally, leaders need to act on the basis of principled beliefs.

Be Not Afraid

Often when I pray, I choose a phrase from the day's gospel reading, which I repeat prayerfully in silence. Often the phrase ends up shaping and informing my whole day. Some phrases have become inspirational themes for months or even years.

One day, as I was praying the gospel lesson, I chose to dwell on the oft-repeated phrase, "Be not afraid." I was anxious about a pending pastoral visit that evening with parishioners whom I knew to be disgruntled and unhappy. Moreover, as I was praying, another parishioner phoned. She was scheduled to have a counseling session that day with her husband. Their marriage was going through a rough patch, and she needed courage. As I reflected on them, I pictured them and breathed, "Be not afraid." As I reflected on my upcoming visit, I prayed the same for myself. It was a helpful and calming exercise.

"Be not afraid" is a phrase that appears often in the Scriptures. Parker Palmer suggests that this idea is not just a Christian emphasis.

> Fear is so fundamental to the human condition that all the great
> spiritual traditions originate in an effort to overcome its effects

on our lives. With different words, they all proclaim the same core message: "Be not afraid." Though the traditions vary widely in the ways they propose to take us beyond fear, all hold out the same hope: we can escape fear's paralysis and enter a state of grace where encounters with otherness will not threaten us but will enrich our work and our lives.[24]

These religious recommendations are not pie-in-the-sky naïveté intended to distract us from real problems. "Be not afraid," Palmer notes, does not mean "that we should not *have* fears" but "that we do not need to *be* our fears, quite a different proposition." I like that distinction between *having* fears and *being* fearful. *Having* fear means that we can act from inner resources rather than being driven by inner fear.

Our fears and anxieties often compel us in unhelpful directions. I see this tendency in the curious story of Jesus stilling the storm (Mark 4:35-41). Jesus, you may recall, was sleeping in the stern of the boat when a storm arose and almost swamped the craft. Not surprisingly, the disciples were terrified and thought they were about to perish. In great desperation they awoke Jesus. "Why are you afraid?" Jesus asked.

Metropolitan Anthony, Eastern Orthodox churchman and scholar, has an interesting take on this story. He believes that the disciples' desperate question to Jesus—"Teacher, do you not care that we are perishing?"—was not just a cry for help.

> First of all they want him to share their suffering. They want him to be as anxious as they are. They think he will not help them unless he shares their anxiety.[25]

While Jesus does in fact help them, he shares neither their anxiety nor their panic. He remains serene and centered. He solves the problem by throwing his own serenity onto the storm: "Peace! Be still."

CHAPTER 8

Solace and Counsel in Fierce Landscapes

> *The light, seen in the icons of Saint Catherine's Monastery [in the Sinai desert], comes not from beyond human flesh and the suffering to which it is heir, but in and through the experience of pain. The icons convey a profound sense of God's grandeur coming through the broken flesh of Christ and the lives of the saints.*
>
> —Belden Lane, *The Solace of Fierce Landscapes*

In an evocative book,[1] Lane makes the point over and again that God meets us, works with us, comforts us, and helps us to grow in places we least expect—places of pain, brokenness, disappointment, frustration, and disillusion. That truth applies also to all we have been addressing.

While dealing with difficult behavior can be—not surprisingly—difficult, nevertheless we can do it with faithfulness and faith in God's unlikely work.

Pain and Anxiety

Once when I was on retreat at a monastery, I made a serious mistake: I called the "outside world" and learned some disheartening personal news. At the end of the phone call I looked across the familiar room where I had been many times and saw a little quotation on the wall that I had never noticed before. The 14th-century German mystic Meister Eckhart said: "Whatever happens to you is the best possible thing for your salvation."

Now that's not a statement that I would cite lightly in pastoral counseling with others. Nevertheless, I recognize the Eckhart approach as being in tune with a spiritual yieldedness and self-abandonment that are in keeping with my own beliefs. I decided to embrace that Eckhart quote, and indeed that sad experience (like so many other hard experiences) proved to be the best possible thing for my salvation and growth.

A major issue in achieving a nonanxious presence is increasing the tolerance of pain, both one's own and that of others. Much anxious behavior in emotional systems is a reaction to the pain that people feel about too much uncertainty, too much ambiguity, too much difference and diversity, too much distance, or too much closeness.

People have different capacities, thresholds, or comfort zones for dealing with pain. Anxious people have a low tolerance. Conversely, people who are more differentiated or more highly motivated and less dependent have higher thresholds.

When systems undergo changes or disruptions, there is often a homeostatic "Change back!" reaction. When our church of 100 experienced an influx of 40 newcomers in a year, a major conflict erupted, driving away some newcomers and even some "old-timers" until the congregation returned to approximately its previous size. Change can be painful, but it is most painful when we are not flexible.

Often our reaction to pain is to get rid of it. But pain is not the problem; it is a pointer to *real* problems and can direct the way to health. If we deal with pain merely by alleviating symptoms as quickly as possible through pain-killers, we risk overlooking the problems that cause the pain. Those who suffer from leprosy lose the capacity to suffer pain and may be unaware of injuries or physical problems.

Pain can move us toward health. I struggle to keep up a physical exercise regimen. (When I get the urge to exercise, I like Mark Twain's advice about lying down until it goes away!) Nevertheless, I know that the "no pain, no gain" rule applies to health: I cannot expect to keep fit unless I subject my body to some physical stress.

Learning from pain is risky for the status quo. Scott Peck believes we live in a "pain-avoiding culture."[2] Some parishioners urge avoidance of pain. Some complain if churches mention hard realities (injustice, abuse, sin). They long for worship that cheers, uplifts, and inspires. But healthiness require facing and paying attention to pain.

When leaders are caught up in alleviating others' pain, they can easily be held hostage to others' anxious emotional agenda. This position may show our own low threshold of tolerating pain. Systemic change is not brought about by capitulating to others' pain. If we do not allow people to live with their pain, we do not help them increase their tolerance for pain either. "Those who focus only on comfort, on relieving pain, or filling another's need, tend to forget that another's need may be *not* to have their needs fulfilled."[3]

Pain can tempt us to find the quickest way for alleviation. But pain can also alert us to the fact that something is awry and that therefore changes need to be made. Pain can have the potential of helping us find healthy ways to adapt.

> In psychotherapy, people adapt more successfully to their environments . . . by facing painful circumstances and developing new attitudes and behaviors. They learn to distinguish reality from fantasy, resolve internal conflicts, and put harsh events into perspective. They learn to live with things that cannot be changed and take responsibility for those that can. By improving their ability to reflect, strengthening their tolerance for frustration, and understanding their own blind spots and patterns of resistance to facing problems, they improve their general adaptive capacity for future challenge.[4]

When leaders are faced with pain in the system, their duty is to help the system respond in ways that mean health and growth, not merely try to find a way back to the homeostatic "good old days."

Yet leadership is contrary to what many expect. "In public life, people generally look to their authorities to solve problems with a minimum of pain, and where pain must be endured, they often expect their officials to find somebody else to bear the costs."[5] How often we see this behavior in elections. Candidates do not campaign promising to make hard and costly changes. I have never heard a politician promise to make us pay high taxes and reorient our lifestyles radically to address the growing environmental crisis. Rather, we hear smooth commitments of our how lives will be improved. If anyone must pay, it is someone else: the undeserving poor, the coddled criminals, the government bureaucrats. And how often we voters want our taxes cut but with no accompanying decrease in services.

But such election tactics do not invite or promote good leadership. Leaders help groups to grow by challenging them to grow in tolerance of pain. Thus nonanxious leaders know how to ask questions, tolerate ambiguity, encourage creativity, and decline to settle for quick fixes.

The Anxiety of Triangulation

Triangling is both a major sign of anxiety and a way that people deal with anxiety. When the anxiety between two parties is unbearable for one party, that party takes those anxieties to a third party, possibly talking about the other to someone else or intensifying a relationship with a third party. Extramarital affairs, gossip, and overwork are among the varieties of triangling. While triangling is a way to reduce personal anxiety, it increases anxiety in the system. Often the third party does not know how to respond to the triangling.

Our point here is that leaders must exercise caution in triangled relationships. Pastors are in a prime position to be triangled. Family members or church members come to us for help in dealing with others. We hear complaints about others. Our pulpit remarks may be interpreted (sometimes accurately) as comments about a particular person. Leaders should also know that triangles often prevent change and growth.

Triangles are inevitable, especially in our line of work. And not all are unhealthy. If a marriage partner goes for therapy, a triangle is created that can ultimately prove therapeutic and helpful. Triangles are not necessarily destructive so long as they are temporary and not rigid.

Yet working in and with triangles is one of our most difficult challenges. Family-systems training and awareness are crucial. A therapist, supervisor, or other kind of coach might appropriately help us see the many kinds of triangles that we can be drawn into.

Being a nonanxious presence in a triangle can help reduce anxiety, so long as one also remains present and connected. Sometimes we need to avoid triangles, and sometimes we need to exit from them. Earlier, we noted some ways that congregations can respond to unhealthy triangles and encourage people to engage in direct relationships. It is important for pastors to learn the same skills.

Dealing with triangles is not easy, but leaders have no choice.

The Hazards of Defensiveness

Defensiveness, one response to pain, and an instance of being too focused on others, can make us oversensitive to criticism. Menno Epp studied terminated pastors and noted that pastors often respond defensively to projections and accusations. Defensive behavior (cut-off or withdrawal) usually creates more problems.[6]

Yet many strong reactions that seem to be directed at us are actually projections. An excellent description of projection to pastors comes from James Dittes. He compares it to overhearing a one-sided conversation in another room.

> The words sound strange, a bit off focus, not really directed to you . . . "I wish you wouldn't play your records so loud,". . . when you don't . . . play records at all. You start to defend yourself, to straighten out the speaker, to explain how wrong he is . . . Then you walk into the speaker's room and discover that he is not talking to you at all; he is on the telephone. Suddenly you can drop your defensiveness, empathize with the speaker, join him in his complaint against the loud records. Being a minister is very much like that—with the special complication that people are often looking right at you instead of talking into the telephone. But what is happening is exactly the same: People only *seem* to be talking to you when, in fact, they are dealing with somebody else and they need your help to do that. Even though you are in the room where you know you belong, . . . they are really talking on the telephone to somebody else and they need you by their side, in their room, while they do that.[7]

The problem is in personalizing projections, and in thinking that they are about us when they are really about the relationships of the person doing the projecting. We do not bring health when we relate to the projections as if they were accurate. Being defensive is a sure way to raise our anxiety. Even people's explicit anger shows more about them than about us.

Ronald Heifetz reminds us that people respond and react to our roles, our actions as leaders, and the perspectives we represent. We need to distinguish between ourselves and our role. He provides a helpful example:

> Most parents know that when their teenage son slams the door in their faces, he is working on the task of separation that accompanies growing up. Though they may be upset with his behavior, they will usually know better than to take it personally. Their son is angry less with them as individuals than with the role they play as

parents. . . . If the parents do take the anger personally, their response will likely be off the mark. They may scream back, sulk, or wall themselves off. Based on a misinterpretation of their son's behavior (He is angry with *us*), they will not be able to give what their son needs next.[8]

Heifetz points out that such realizations are important, as they enable leaders "not to be misled by . . . emotions into taking statements and events personally that may have little to do with [us]."

More than not being defensive, we must learn how to invite and be open to challenge, criticism, and dissent. Once I was short-listed for a position that I dearly wanted. The job went to another candidate. Shortly after that process, I was at an event and saw the chair of the personnel committee that had interviewed me. I knew I could be civil but did not go out of my way to speak to him. I was surprised when he immediately approached me, engaged me in conversation, asked how the process had felt, and wondered whether I had any issues with him. His approach dissolved and disarmed any awkwardness, and after that I always felt free to speak with him and enjoy his company as I had before the interview process. I resolved to learn from him.

Not being defensive in the face of assaults and accusations may be difficult, but it is essential. The reactivity of others can feed on *our* defensiveness. Anxious reactions can heighten the very phenomena that make us anxious.

A wonderful story tells of an alternative to defensiveness practiced by the curé d'Ars who eventually became known as St. John Vianney. He was not well educated and was "irritatingly zealous." Eventually people in his parish launched a petition complaining about his lack of qualifications and "declaring him 'unfit' to hold his post." The curé was eager to see this petition, understandably enough. When he finally saw it, he promptly signed it![9]

Turning Critics Into Teachers

Most church leaders soon realize that criticism, as painful as it may be, comes with the territory. Thus an essential skill is the ability to deal well with inevitable criticism.

Since criticism can feel like rejection, it might seem to be a distancing maneuver. But criticism is really a form of *pursuit,* a behavior that tries to draw us away from differentiation. It feels as if criticism is pushing us away, but that is not its purpose.

> Whenever someone gets under our skin, we are infected with anxiety. If we are reactive to a pursuer, the pursuit behavior achieves its goal: connection. Strange as it sounds, the critic wants to be close. After all, if we can't be close through play, ecstasy, touch, and nurture, our only option to accomplish closeness is through angry outbursts, specious charges, or harsh accusations. People feel close to us when they know we are thinking about them. *What* we think is not as important as *that* we are thinking about them.[10]

That realization may help us to deal a little more compassionately and tenderly with those who criticize.

Here too the distinction between role and self is vital. Otherwise we can internalize difficulties and conflicts. That reaction is problematic for many reasons: It personalizes problems that are not personal, it deflects attention from the real issue, and it increases defensiveness, reinforcing the problem.

It is imperative that pastoral leaders not just allow criticism but deliberately make room for it. Earlier we noted the need for reliable grievance procedures. Such procedures welcome criticisms and vent concerns that could grow into potentially explosive problems. Healthy churches are open to dissent and criticism. In fact, we do well to think of our critics as a "loyal opposition," essential to the healthy operation of our church.

We need to welcome criticism even when we feel attacked. Says Speed Leas: "A piece of advice that I often give pastors who are under siege from battlesome people is that they *respond to challenges by affirming the value of raising criticisms*, that they even thank . . . scrappy board members for surfacing concerns that couldn't have been dealt with if they had not brought them up at this time."[11] Critical people are fearful, just as the people criticized are fearful. We need to respond to criticisms first by affirming the *appropriateness* of having criticisms raised.

We need also to *listen* to criticisms and consider whether they are appropriate. What can we learn here? Do we need to change a direction or offer an apology? We need to take a learning stance toward the criticisms raised.

Pastoral consultant John Savage does much work on dealing with criticism, including "fogging" ("naming the truth in another's critical statements") and "negative inquiry" ("coaching your critic to criticize you in specifics, rather than in generalities"). The latter is challenging. When criticized, we can ask productive questions for specifics about what is criticized. Savage's methods can help us have a "sense of control while being criticized. Usually, our emotions fire off, and we want to run, avoid, deny, or defend." Such skills reduce our anxiety when we feel attacked.[12]

If attacks are particularly heated, Leas tells us other things to consider as well.[13]

- Do not attack the other's arguments, but show what you have done well.
- Listen to what is said, but it also appropriate for you to share your perceptions.
- Work on changing how problems are defined.
- While the temptation might be always to express differences, it is wise to give in on things that are not important.
- If things really get tense or problematic, bring a third party in to assist in the process.

As Leas says: "Keep moving in a way that invites the others to share, but at the same time assumes that you are going to maintain fully your power, rights, and responsibilities in the situation."[14]

We can reframe an attitude that sees criticism as inherently negative to one that views it as intrinsically worthwhile. Savage calls this a way "to turn your critic into your teacher, rather than your enemy."[15] While this is not always fun, let alone easy, it is a way of learning about oneself and helping one to make changes if one so chooses. No matter how the complaint is presented or even whether our perceptions differ, it is crucial that we try to listen for the information we can glean.

College administrator Norma Cole McKinnon recommends four steps for taking criticism well.[16]

- First, listen attentively to what is said and communicated (including non-verbal messages), without interrupting and without using the time to formulate your response.

- Second, paraphrase what you hear: This clarifies information and helps the other feel heard.
- Third, graciously ask for specific details.
- Finally, find something together about which you can agree.

If we have trouble sorting out the accuracy, relevance, or appropriateness of criticisms, it is good to consult with others. A good reality check can be the board, the personnel committee, a trusted friend, a therapist, or a supervisor.

James Sparks, professor at the University of Wisconsin–Madison, notes that after being attacked we often brood in defensive ways with self-blaming, obsessing, or fantasizing.[17] He recommends four steps for dealing with defensive reactions.

- First, acknowledge to yourself that you are in a poor frame of mind.
- Second, name the negative feelings or resentment you feel toward your critic.
- Third, interrupt the brooding with exercise, pleasant mental visualization, a short walk, a lunch with a friend, or some other "five-minute vacation."
- Finally, tell the situation to a friend.

Giving Criticism

The other side of receiving criticism is giving it, which can be equally awkward, provocative, anxiety-raising, and painful. Just as leaders need to expect and welcome criticism, we also have a responsibility at times to offer criticism and hold others accountable. Criticism is often done poorly as attacks, put-downs, or disrespect. Such criticism is destructive and helps no one. It can also backfire: Those criticized may believe themselves incapable of change or improvement.

According to Allen C. Filley, writer on conflict resolution, self-examination is in order before we plunge into making criticisms:

It is a good idea to check why one really wants to give such information to another. Where the giver is in effect saying, "I'm doing this for your own good," he frequently means, "It gives me pleasure to be able to tell you these things." Self-gratification is not the intended purpose of feedback. . . . If the process is to be effective, . . . the senders should be legitimately interested in helping the receivers understand themselves by providing insights into their behavior.[18]

The challenge is to deliver criticism as helpful teachers and encouragers. We can confront, criticize, and acknowledge differences in ways that invite all parties to grow.

Several important themes emerge in learning to be good critics.

- *Focus on actions.* Do not focus on the other's character.
- *Be affirming and respectful.* If one does not compliment (affirming what the other does well), do not expect the criticism to be heard. In offering criticism, use language that is descriptive rather than judgmental.
- *Be specific.* Rather than speak generally, discuss a particular incident that needs to be addressed; it is demoralizing not to hear specifics. Confine discussion to the specifics on the agenda.
- *Offer solutions and focus on things that can be changed.* It is not enough to say what is wrong. Suggest ideas for how the problem can be addressed; offer ideas and options. Invite the other person to come up with suggestions as well.
- *Be present.* It is important to meet face-to-face, preferably in private. Letters, memos, and E-mail messages are too easily misconstrued or misunderstood. Phone calls sometimes work, but one misses the physical messages and expressions.
- *Be calm and nonanxious.* Your tone of voice and body language—as well as your words—need to be nonthreatening
- *Be sensitive.* Do not be so focused on delivering your message that you are not aware how this news might be received.
- *Be open to feedback.* Give the other an opportunity to tell his or her perspective on the matter.
- *Close with praise and a plan.* Finish with an affirmation for the person's willingness to discuss the issues with you, and make clear any follow-up that is needed.

Difficult Behavior as Opportunity

Sometimes when people reflect on difficulties, circumstances they would not choose, they cite a cliché: "It was a learning experience." I wish I could learn all I need by reading books in comfortable solitude. "For most people growth and learning . . . happen not when things are going well but when previous concepts about themselves have been confounded and new insights are necessary to make sense of the changed world."[19]

Earlier we noted the problem of the victim mentality. Sometimes people are mired in the perspective of feeling victimized. While problems can overwhelm us, they can also be challenging opportunities to learn. When confronted with difficult circumstances, we have a choice. It is said that a Chinese symbol for "crisis" includes symbols for both "danger" and "opportunity." Relational problems can be opportunities to work on the relationship. Even failures offer the chance to learn.

This opportunity to learn is evident in some of the literature on dismissals of pastors. Many who write about this experience see it as a time of unprecedented growth. Even so, Leas notes that most terminated clergy he studied learned nothing from their experience but "got stuck in bitterness, denial, blaming, and vituperation."[20]

Dittes invented a felicitous phrase, "the call in the disruption."[21] He suggests that when we pay attention to the roadblocks and detours, we may discover a call from God. Henri Nouwen tells a revealing story.

> While visiting the University of Notre Dame, . . . I met an older experienced professor who had spent most of his life there. And while we strolled over the beautiful campus, he said with a certain melancholy in his voice, "You know, . . . my whole life I have been complaining that my work was constantly interrupted, until I discovered that my interruptions were my work."[22]

In our busy society, we are in constant haste. We expect to reach people instantly or at least be able to leave a message. A pastoral colleague gets flak from parishioners because she refuses to have an answering machine. But Nouwen poses an alternative response to barriers and interruptions.

> What if our interruptions are in fact our opportunities, . . . challenges . . . by which growth takes place . . . ? What if the events

of our history are molding us as a sculptor molds . . . clay, and if it is only in a careful obedience to these molding hands that we can discover our real vocation and become mature people?[23]

Nouwen made this challenge real and personal for me years ago, after I experienced a bitter church conflict. He stressed that my losses were great. Experience of betrayal in the church is devastating, he said. But he noted that Jesus experienced betrayal by a friend and John of the Cross was imprisoned by fellow monks. He observed that all mystics had suffered. This experience, he said, could also free me.

Dare we trust that there can be purpose even in difficult behavior? When faced with difficulties, I am tempted to cry out and complain like the prophet Elijah, "I alone am left" (1 Kings 19:10). I might wish for someone else's challenges but "by definition, no one gets the problem he or she can handle."[24] After all, if we could handle it, it would not be a problem!

An amusing story about a noted teacher and spiritual master illustrates the value of learning from difficult behavior.

> In the spiritual community that G. I. Gurdjieff led . . . , an old man lived . . . who was the personification of difficulty—irritable, messy, fighting with everyone, and unwilling to clean up or help at all. No one got along with him. Finally, after many frustrating months of trying to stay with the group, the old man left for Paris. Gurdjieff followed him and tried to convince him to return, but it had been too hard, and the man said no. At last Gurdjieff offered the man a very big monthly stipend if he returned. How could he refuse? When he returned everyone was aghast, and on hearing that he was being paid (while they were being charged a lot to be there), the community was up in arms. Gurdjieff laughed and explained: "This man is like yeast for bread." He said, "Without him here you would never really learn about anger, irritability, patience, and compassion. That is why you pay me, and I hire him."[25]

Crises in ministries can be a way to growth, transformation, and productive ministry.

Several times I heard Henri Nouwen quote his friend Parker Palmer, who said, "We might define true community as that place where the person you least want to live with always lives."[26] That reminds us that those whose behavior we find difficult also offer us the greatest opportunities for growth. Nouwen says it this way:

> The one you least want to live with is the one who reminds you of that part of yourself that is most wounded and most in need of healing. He makes you aware that you have not reached your destination yet, but have to keep moving on in an unceasing process of confession and forgiveness.[27]

Christian faith is rooted in the power and hope of the Resurrection, when life came out of death and hate, the greatest of obstacles. The difficult behavior Jesus faced was costly, but it was not the end. We are called to be creative problem-solvers in the face of disruptive and difficult situations. Do not forget Friedman's wise counsel: "The major factor that promotes survival in any environment is the same that has led to the evolution of our species since creation: an organism's response to challenge."[28]

There *is* solace in fierce landscapes.

CHAPTER 9

Tuning Our Own Harpstrings

A man drove through an unfamiliar neighborhood that he considered shady. Its residents were of a different race and class than he. And sure enough, as soon as he drove down the first block (having carefully locked his doors), he noticed that people on the sidewalks were yelling and gesturing at him as he drove along. The further he drove, the more outraged and outrageous their angry communication sounded. This behavior confirmed all that he had suspected and disliked about "these kinds of people."

But then he realized he had been driving the wrong way down a one-way street! People were trying to draw his attention to his unsafe wrong-way driving. If only he had paid more attention to his own actions!

It is tempting to blame or feel attacked by others, to assume that others or their behavior are our problem, to believe that our well-being or peace of mind could be assured *if only* others would cooperate. All that we have studied shows us that ultimately *we* are primarily responsible only for ourselves.

Appropriate Focus on Self

Focusing on and blaming *other* people and claiming the role of victim is an insidious form of anxiety. While we may recognize the difficult behavior of parishioners, leaders often play this game too. Pastors tell many martyrdom stories. I know, because I have often done so. Speed Leas believes that when a terminated "pastor places blame entirely on other persons or groups," he or she shows a major sign of interpersonal incompetence.[1]

Seeing oneself as a victim inhibits growth. We refuse responsibility and attribute blame elsewhere. With such an attitude, we block our capacity to grow. Moreover, when we regard ourselves as victims, we often act destructively and hurt ourselves more.

But life does not have to be this way. We can make choices. We do not have to remain mired in the past. Bad and malicious things may happen to good people, but we must make choices about what we do with those events.

The flip side of victim behavior is to see others as *enemies*. Focusing on others indicates fusion rather than differentiation; it assumes that the other controls our reactions and emotions. In family therapy, focusing on others is not helpful or productive. Seeing others as enemies is a way of blaming them when our hopes or ideals are not met.

A victim mentality and an other-focused outlook are anxious and irresponsible. They often involve triangling: A victim/martyr complains to a rescuer about the persecutor. Rather than look to others, we should more appropriately examine ourselves.

In his lectures, Leas encouraged us to analyze what *we* gain from conflict. Why are we in it? What is my role? This difficult work may require the help of a therapist or a close, trusted friend. We need to ask ourselves what the payoff is for us in this conflict. Why do we keep it going? Perhaps because we cannot bear to see a relationship end, we stay in a conflictual relationship. Perhaps we do not know or believe that there can be anything better than a conflicted relationship. Women who return to abusive marriages may feel that being in a relationship is more important than not being hurt. Perhaps we enjoy seeing others as villains. Perhaps we enjoy exerting power.

A pastor was having difficulty in his parish. He saw a therapist for several sessions, all the while complaining. The therapist finally said, "It's obvious that the church is screwing you. What interests me is why you keep dropping your pants."

Rather than act like victims or complain about enemies or oppressors, we can make the choice to grow and change. One of the most important lessons we can learn in relational difficulties is that we cannot change or control others. We are capable only of changing ourselves and caring for ourselves. By refusing to expect others to change, we take away one more anxiety-inducer.

Our work is not complete until we understand how *we* contribute to undesirable situations and how *our* behavior can be changed.

Reorienting Our Perspectives

One great challenge in appropriately focusing on ourselves also involves taking responsibility for our attitude toward others and their behavior. Beware of concluding too quickly that the beloved (or not-so-beloved) antagonist in your church is pathological. Have you made every effort to understand what makes an adversary "tick" and why he or she acts out?

Once I was preoccupied with how a certain church family treated me. I could not let go of the memories of what that family did. Worried about my anger and resentment, I wondered whether I was getting stuck in bitterness. Alas, I could not try to forget these people because I drove by their house every day! (Avoiding it would have meant adding unnecessary miles to my daily driving.)

At a conference with church consultant John Savage, I had a meal with him and shared my dilemma. He led me through a simple exercise by asking these questions: Can you describe how you perceive them? Can you describe how *they* perceive the world, you, and others in church? Can you describe how others perceive them? Such distancing perspectives help us to be more objective and less reactive.

Timothy O'Connell, ethics professor at Loyola University, describes a neuro-linguistic programming (NLP) method that can be helpful (and is similar to what Savage—an NLP proponent—did). He discusses the problem of how we regard past experiences that were painful and negative. One can practice *dissociation* by looking again at that negative experience.

> In imagination, [NLP practitioners] . . . lead the participant to view that scene from any point of view other than their own. That is, they . . . encourage the participant to dissociate from that past experience. Doing this produces an almost immediate reduction in the negative feelings associated with the image.[2]

O'Connell notes that the converse of this method can also be helpful. Rather than trying to dissociate from negative images and memories, one visualizes positive and hopeful images. "Doing this sort of thing repeatedly . . . can lead to a deepening of positive feeling and reduction of negative feeling." This is also one of the good fruits of a healthy prayer life. Indeed, O'Connell connects NLP with Ignatian contemplation.

The Need for Self-Examination

Being differentiated means taking responsibility for oneself and staying focused on oneself. When we feel as though we are the uncomfortable focus for others' difficult behavior, our temptation is to focus on others and blame them for troubles. But the challenge is for us to work on our own growth and self-awareness.

We must ask ourselves whether in fact *we* are the cause of the problems. Perhaps our antagonism and hostility contribute to the difficulties we endure. Conrad Weiser's *Healers—Harmed and Harmful* is a sobering reminder of the kinds of problems that can emerge when pastors are not self-aware. When we encounter disruptive behavior or our emotionality is rising, the first thing we need to do is pay attention to ourselves.

We can grow more self-aware by paying attention to those whose behavior we label "difficult." They tell us more about ourselves than anything else. We need to ask, "What is it about this behavior that pushes my buttons? Does it remind me of someone who troubled me in the past? Am I afraid I may be or become like them?"

Early in my years as a pastor, I got into a fierce conflict with a parishioner. My therapist kept asking an irritating question: "Why do this person's actions bothers you so much?" I was annoyed because it seemed obvious what was troublesome. Would not anyone be bothered by it? In fact, no. Something in my composition was unsettled by behavior that did not necessarily bother others. The challenge was for me to learn and grow.

Just as we try to turn critics into teachers, even the most difficult behavior can become a learning experience. People who behave in a difficult manner can teach us. As we understand ourselves and others better, we can grow in compassion.

Preoccupation with certain parishioners is an alarm signal that it may be time to seek help. Others include sleeplessness (especially that caused by preoccupation with the problem), talking incessantly about the situation with family or friends, depression, anger, indecisiveness, fatigue, weight gain or loss, fearfulness. All these are signs that something is amiss and that it may be appropriate to enter therapy. Self-awareness can be increased by conversations with trusted friends, supervision from a mentor, participation in a supervised clinical experience, work with a peer group, or sessions with a spiritual director.

We do not pursue such knowledge merely for the sake of its own pursuit. We are manipulated by our feelings if we are not aware of them. Says

Daniel Goleman: "People with greater certainty about their feelings are better pilots of their lives, have a surer sense of how they really feel about personal decisions."[3] Awareness of emotions is a first step to gaining control over impulses. Such awareness can put us—and not our emotions or our reactivity—in charge.

Ronald Heifetz regards self-awareness as a major requirement for leaders. He has a marvelous phrase for self-awareness, self-understanding, and self-control: "tuning one's own harpstrings." It is helpful for us to reflect regularly on our lives. He notes that

> we learn by reflecting on daily actions, successes and failures, of ourselves and others. In particular, we can learn from those habits that repeatedly get us into trouble and from those behaviors that surprise us. They often provide clues to our own peculiar mesh of internal drives and social forces.[4]

A classic spiritual discipline, *consciousness examen*, is an excellent method for regular self-examination, noting patterns, habits, and directions in one's life.

Warning Signs and Perceptions

While the need for self-awareness cannot be overstated, I do not advocate or recommend naïve navel-gazing. A savvy leader pays attention to what is going on and may notice early warning signs of trouble ahead.

Often an early sign of serious unhappiness is a dramatic change in the involvement of an active member. John Savage's work as a consultant began first with his study of inactive, bored, and apathetic members who withdrew for a host of reasons. People start on the dropout track after an anxiety-provoking event (which may or may not be church-related). Next, they signal their anxiety in some way. If the signal is not responded to, then they display anger in the form of either apathy or boredom. Next, they withdraw. After their withdrawal, a six-to-eight-week period of opportunity remains when it is still possible to connect with such folk and help them to re-engage with the church.[5]

If someone's pattern of participation changes dramatically, the pastor or some other church caregiver needs to respond promptly. (Keeping track of Sunday attendance is one way to detect changes in attendance patterns.)

I often find that lay leaders hesitate to follow up on inactive members. Ironically, the longer a person has been part of our congregation, the harder it is to follow up. When a family attended for a year, attempted to oust the pastor, and left in a huff, the church immediately made many efforts to draw the people back. When a husband and wife, both in their 80s, suddenly stopped attending, even though he had been part of the church from birth and was a direct descendant of the church's founders, no formal follow-up ensued.

Churches seem to be uneasy about prying into a parishioner's privacy. People hesitate to explore anything that might prove unpleasant or might surface unruly emotions. But responding to withdrawals is part of our responsibility.

> To leave someone to their own initiative in disclosing how they feel is the same . . . as allowing everyone to determine when and whether they are, in fact, physically ill. . . . [A] caring question by a concerned Christian brother or sister need not be construed as meddling. Would the same be said of a doctor when he asks personal questions in inquiring about his patients?[6]

When people start to withdraw, they are already indicating some possible anxiety. Thus *how* we deal with them is important. By asking sincere and interested questions and showing interest in the other's situation, one can have a calming effect.

A parishioner resigned from a major involvement in the church. I asked to meet with her. She was anxious that I might pressure her or criticize her decision. Instead, I asked simply and neutrally, "What's going on for you these days?" Later, she said that that conversation was a gift.

Withdrawing from church can be a passive-aggressive way of dealing with hostility or anger. Rather than confronting directly, members withdraw. In heavily enmeshed churches or in small "single-cell" congregations, withdrawal is sometimes used as a threat to get the group to behave according to the disgruntled person's wishes. In the small churches I have worked with, the worry that someone might leave has consistently been one of people's greatest fears.

While we need to connect with and visit those who withdraw or threaten to withdraw, we must be firm with such tactics. To cave in to ultimatums about leaving is to err on the side of fusion rather than moving in the healthier direction of differentiation. Differentiation includes the ability to let others go.

There can be good, healthy reasons to withdraw. That is another reason why follow-up "exit interviews" are helpful. Until we check with someone, Daniel Bagby suggests, we cannot know why they left, whether the reason is healthy or not, or whether they might come back.

> A member may choose to leave a congregation over some issues, and his leaving need not be decried as destructive. There are occasions when a member clearly senses that his position and that of the body is . . . divergent. He may then exercise God's will in retaining the sense of unity of the fellowship by withdrawing himself. His stewardship and outlook can effectively be used by God in another place and perhaps more effectively be channeled by another congregation. Pastor and caring leaders sometimes need to bless this departure as inspired by God.[7]

Emphases on community and togetherness make it especially difficult to deal with those who leave or threaten to do so. My present rural congregation is almost two centuries old and has experienced two major church spits and numerous theological battles and rifts along the way, including severe recent conflicts. These explosive conflicts indicate that we have a problem with differentiation. We are so unable to tolerate differences and diversity that splitting or cutting off is a major way to deal with our anxiety.

There are other danger signs that we might note: decline in financial giving, strident positions taken by key people, rumors of dissatisfaction, circulation of petitions, anonymous letters of complaint posted on bulletin boards or sent to the church office, lobbying efforts for the pastor's dismissal, and the snubbing of one parishioner by another.[8]

Warning signs are all only alarm signals or "presenting problems"; i.e., *symptoms* of problems. They alert us that problems exist and need to be addressed.

It is not enough to pay attention to what we perceive or think is happening. It is important to test perceptions with reality checks. When one family stopped attending, I wondered whether they were angry about something. Perhaps so, but my anxieties were allayed when I learned that they now attended a Mennonite church much nearer their home, a church that had children in the same age range as their own children.

There are several reasons to check perceptions. For one, perceptions are often self-fulfilling. Too often what we think we see is what we end up getting, and our perceptions helped make this possible. Not only our perceptions but also our reactive descriptions and language can become self-ful-filling.

Another reason to check perceptions is that even with our facts right, it is notoriously easy to get our perceptions and interpretations wrong. So often dissent, unhappiness, and anger are expressed in ambiguous ways. Pastors are often not especially good at interpreting symptoms. Early in my pastoring, my mood would swing up or down with Sunday-morning attendance. I assumed that each Sunday's attendance (never mind holidays, vacations, illnesses, and travel) was a commentary on me. It took me a long time to convince myself that routine fluctuations in attendance are not about the pastor.

As you see warning signs, remember not to be caught up in the anxiety-provoking potentials of specific details. Rather, look at the congregation as a system, and study what the warning signs tell you about the system as a whole.

A systems approach reminds us not to take everything personally. When our Sunday attendance swelled by 40 percent, I was tempted to take credit. When, a few years later, attendance returned to approximately its former size, I was tempted to take the blame. Systems analysis showed that the reduction in size was a homeostatic response. A major conflict immediately after the increased attendance was a mechanism to regulate our size. Systems perspectives call us to look not so much at the *specifics* of what seems wrong as to understand why this incident happened *now*. While our church needed to address the conflict, the conflict was part of a larger systemic picture.

When I perceive worrisome circumstances, a first line of reality-checking is with our church's pastoral-support committee. This group helps me analyze what goes on in the church. Their analysis helps me interpret and understand. Often, they know simple details that put a completely different spin on what I see.

Another major resource for me in understanding the church and its symptoms was a pastors' study group. For the first hour of each session we studied and reflected on books explaining family systems. In the second hour, we took turns presenting a case study from our own ministry and analyzing it with what we had learned. For years I have also been part of prayer groups with pastors who engage in frank sharing and discernment.

At other times, my reality checks have been provided by supervisors, therapists, spiritual directors, friends, or colleagues.

More than ever, when difficult signs loom on the horizon, leaders need to take the stance of researchers, trying to understand the situation. The very process of trying to understand, a "research stance," calms down the whole system. Simply asking questions helps everyone to get away from emotionality and reactivity. The purpose is to move us away from our instinctual and unthinking emotive reactions.

Self-Care

We are subject to many demands and expectations, internal and external. Without proper self-care and a strong sense of direction, we are in deep, deep trouble.

A leader's work is stressful. That is a given. What is not a given is how we choose to respond to it. Stress taxes us, but responsible professional clergy will be mindful of good ways to care for themselves.

Self-care is particularly important in relation to the subject at hand because dealing with difficult behavior and intense conflict can be especially draining. Health and stability should not be assumed or taken for granted. It is imperative that pastors practice self-care to protect their ability to continue being empathic in their work. This is particularly important when we feel attacked by difficult behavior. When I spoke to Nouwen about some of my frustrations in pastoring, he bluntly said: "If people are using you, find your center."

Leaders sometimes deny their right to self-care by complaining (or even boasting) of busyness. Busyness is the number-one complaint I hear from pastors (and indeed, from most parishioners). Edwin Friedman is suspicious of busy overfunctioning and considers it doubly anxious: not only does it show dependency; it creates dependency. Not only does it manifest anxiety; it also increases anxiety.[9]

In the face of difficult behavior and conflict in the congregation, several elements are crucial for a pastor's self-preservation and care.

- Have clear job descriptions and get expectations out on the table. Many churches operate without clearly stated expectations. It is a pastor's responsibility to get expectations named and negotiated.
- Maintain good family relationships and clear communication. Do family-of-origin work if you have not done so before.

- Keep good and open working relationships with officers and informal leaders in the congregation and with fellow staff.
- Nurture friendships outside the congregation so that you are not wholly dependent on the church for socializing and support.
- Take regular vacations. Many pastors do not take even the vacation time to which they are entitled!
- Meet with peers, either in your denomination or ecumenically, for prayer, sharing, or recreation. Build a support system when things are calm: I have found that this task is more difficult during crises. Heifetz notes that we need partners:

Even if the weight of carrying people's hopes and pains may fall mainly . . . on one person's shoulders, leadership cannot be exercised alone. The lone-warrior model of leadership is heroic suicide. Each of us has blind spots that require the vision of others. Each of us has passions that need to be contained by the other.[10]

He recommends two kinds of partners: confidants (to whom we can complain and grieve) and allies (who can help us accomplish our goals).

- Keep a fresh perspective by engaging in further study or continuing education.
- Nurture your spiritual life: Pray regularly, see a spiritual director, and go on retreats.
- Get regular exercise.
- Keep plenty of options open, both for how you act in the church and for moving elsewhere if necessary. We act more calmly when we have more options. The biggest mistakes I made as a pastor were when I could not imagine myself as a pastor anywhere but in the troubled parish I then served. I panicked for fear that I could not stay there, anxiously trying to force changes I felt were needed.
- Relax and get new perspectives through hobbies, art, recreation, and music.
- If things feel overwhelming, see a therapist.
- If the church seems overwhelming, bring in an outside consultant.
- Heifetz also says we need a sanctuary, a place to listen to ourselves. "When serving as the repository of many conflicting aspirations, a person can lose himself in the role by failing to distinguish his inner

voice from the voices that clamor for attention outside"[11] Find safe places to listen to yourself: with a friend, on a walk, during prayer.
*   We also need a sense of mission to motivate and direct us, especially when things are not going well. It helps us deal with failures, risk failures, and make corrections when we fail, and it gives us the freedom to change and try new things.[12]

Self-care is vital in dealing with difficult behavior in the congregation. It keeps us vital and versatile as we face various changes.

Nourishing a Relationship with God

This book has been as practical as possible. At bottom, the problem of difficult behavior is a spiritual issue and calls us to care for our own relationship with God.

During a devastating church conflict, I relearned something I had always claimed to know: I came to a deep realization of God's love. Such a rediscovery may sound strange. After all, as a pastor, I am supposed to be an expert in God's love: proclaiming it to others and knowing it in my own life.

A new friend, Mike, was a tenured professor. In his late 40s, he was doing well in a successful career with a secure future, but felt deeply dissatisfied and unfulfilled. He took a sabbatical and studied at a seminary. The year was so important to him that he resigned his tenured university position, completed a master of divinity degree, and has since taken a country church. At seminary he learned how much God loves him. All of his studies, biblical work, prayer life, counseling, and worship led to a new conversion. Before, he was motivated by guilt, rules, and shame; he had an intrinsically negative view of God. But at seminary he saw how much God loved him and even delighted in him. It was a freeing realization.

Another new friend, Don, taught me a similar lesson. He is 30 years my senior with a wealth of ministry experience. We met providentially as a church conflict was unfolding. A mentor, he walked with me in deeply empathetic ways during my difficult days because years ago he had been through a similar crisis. He overworked, could not deal effectively with a looming church problem, and badly neglected his family. Life got to be too much, and he left his job. He entered a recovery program to deal with his workaholism. He knew he had made a mess of his life: He had given up his job and now faced the risk that he might lose his wife too. He lost vitality for ministry and had to make a difficult choice of facing the truth about himself or continuing to ignore it. This was a time of deeply painful questions.

In the recovery program he realized that he had never lost his place before God. God always loved him and still did. God never stopped. Don may have violated his relationship with God and others, but God still held him in loving tenderness. Don may have gone astray, but he still felt God's loving embrace.

Not surprisingly, he became a pastor again, living and working from the perspective of God's great grace and love. He was much more effective. He still made mistakes and still struggled, but he came a long way. He knew that God's loving grace is the only sure foundation for ministry.

Much of my early ministry was based in something other than love. I worked hard to please God as if to win salvation. But ministry is a grateful response to God's love. I do not need to win God's love; I need only to live it.

I worked hard to win approval and affection from others. But the only ultimately important affection is God's love, and that is already settled. It was achieved not by my merits but by God's grace. Resting in God's love, I detach myself from the traps of relying on the approval or affection of others. In so doing, I begin to love more freely and so am a better pastor.

For a long time I prayed that my children would grow up to be disciples and that they would know joy in that service. Later, I added another petition: "May they always know that they are deeply loved by you."

When I was four, I attended my first vacation Bible school. Ever since, I have been deeply aware of God's relationship with me and have been conscientious about the faith. The song that I learned then, four decades ago, is one that I soon knew by heart, but whose message still nurtures me: "Jesus loves me! This I know."

When I met Henri Nouwen years ago, I talked to him about an experience with burnout. He told me:

> God is calling you to a deep spiritual life. . . . Tenderness can destroy you because you can just be pulled apart, burn out, and the whole thing. But you can also be a mystic. That's what you obviously have to be. To be a mystic, I don't mean anything more than that God is the one who loves you deeply. And that's what you have to trust. And keep trusting, keep trusting, keep trusting.

It seems ironic that my bitter failure better enabled my ministry. Perhaps I should not be surprised: Paul learned this long ago when the Lord said, "My grace is sufficient for you, for my power is made perfect in weakness" (2 Cor. 12:9).

I undertook this work because dealing with difficult behavior in the congregation is one of the biggest and most draining challenges in pastoring. But "draining" does not have to mean debilitating. In fact, facing such difficulties has contributed more to my growth as a person and a pastor than any other hurdles I have encountered. While it is not simple to address difficult behavior, it is possible to do so responsibly.

The Dutch Calvinism of my biological ancestors is too deeply rooted and programmed for me to be mistaken for an optimist. But I am hopeful that churches can be both homes for those whose behavior does not work well in any sphere and places of growth and healing for all who participate.

In closing I offer one more story in which idealism, hope, realism, and possibility all conspired to bring something new to birth.

*****

For one life-changing summer, my wife and I lived in a Catholic Worker community in inner-city Detroit. Our home was an emergency shelter for women, children, and families. As well as attending to the shelter's needs, we helped at a soup kitchen in the neighborhood.

Every Sunday, there was a worship service in the house, and the Eucharist was celebrated, followed by a potluck meal. This event attracted service-oriented believers from across the city, peace-and-justice activists, shelter guests, and soup-kitchen patrons. The services were always memorable.

One regular attender, whom I'll call "Donny," was a homeless man who measured over seven-and-a-half feet tall. (One Catholic worker told me of the difficulty of finding him shoes.) This giant attended every Sunday for many years. He would have loved nothing more than to lead the service, but because of mental problems his skills were limited. Besides, this was a Roman Catholic Eucharist, and only a duly ordained priest could preside.

During the eucharistic liturgy, Donny had an annoying habit of repeating the last phrase of everything the celebrant said. He had heard the liturgy so often that he had practically memorized it. Sometimes he tried to say the prayers and formulas *before* the celebrant did. His habit was distracting and hardly worshipful!

But how does a community committed to compassion and hospitality deal with such a problem? Donny was not mentally equipped for extended reasoning or careful conflict resolution. Besides, you want to be careful about getting into conflict with someone who stands seven-and-a-half feet tall!

There were temptations for the group. Some no doubt wished that Donny would disappear. Some wondered about silencing or evicting him. Resentment and annoyance would have made it easy to resort to criticism, avoidance, name-calling, or labeling. But those who serve in Catholic Worker communities are known for their idealism, and they succumbed to none of these temptations.

The community wrestled with the issue for a long time. The solution was brilliant.

Donny was given one phrase in the service, "Behold the Lamb of God, who takes away the sins of the world." This was his line and no one else's. At the appropriate moment, the celebrant elevated the loaf of bread in silence and waited for Donny to say his line, which he did with gusto, enthusiasm, devotion, and even panache.

Donny got his wish for a meaningful leadership role in the service. He did so without detracting from the ceremonial solemnity for the rest of the worshippers. During the remainder of the service, Donny sat quietly and contentedly, a rare accomplishment at any time in his life!

Donny stood out for many reasons: a freakish physical stature, mental illness, extreme poverty, membership in an oppressed race. It was not easy for this alternative Christian community to know how to include him. Yet its brilliant solution was good for everyone.

*****

May the Spirit that inspired that community's solution continue to inspire *us* as we face our own great challenges in trying to be responsible church leaders.

NOTES

Introduction

1. Michael Smith, "Pastors Under Fire: A Personal Report," *Christian Century* (23 February 1994): 196.

2. Smith, "Pastors Under Fire," 196; Edwin Friedman cited in Peter L. Steinke, *How Your Church Family Works* (Bethesda: Alban, 1993), v.

3. Cited by G. Lloyd Rediger, *Clergy Killers: Guidance for Pastors and Congregations Under Attack* (Inver Grove Heights, Minn.: Logos Productions, 1997), 13.

4. This section relies on Speed B. Leas, *Moving Your Church Through Conflict* (Washington: Alban, 1985), chapter 3.

Chapter 1

1. Stephen R. Covey, *The Seven Habits of Highly Effective People: Powerful Lessons in Personal Change* (New York: Simon & Schuster, 1989), 300-01.

2. In this discussion on the limits of labeling, I relied heavily on Edwin H. Friedman, *Generation to Generation* (New York: Guilford Press, 1985), 56-58, 209.

3. Friedman, *Generation to Generation*, 57.

4. Parker J. Palmer, *The Courage to Teach* (San Francisco: Jossey-Bass, 1998), 42ff.

Chapter 2

1. Kenneth C. Haugk, *Antagonists in the Church* (Minneapolis: Augsburg, 1988), 39.

2. Kenneth Alan Moe, *The Pastor's Survival Manual* (Bethesda, Md.: Alban, 1995), 51-52.

3. Anthony G. Pappas, *Pastoral Stress* (Bethesda, Md.: Alban, 1995), 47.

4. Paul R. Stevens and Phil Collins, *The Equipping Pastor* (Bethesda, Md.: Alban, 1993), 33.

5. Steinke, *How Your Church Family Works*, 59.

6. Steinke, *How Your Church Family Works*, 59.

7. Robert M. Bramson, *Coping with Difficult People* (New York: Doubleday, 1981), 27.

8. Hugh F. Halverstadt, *Managing Church Conflict* (Louisville: Westminster John Knox, 1991), 2.

9. Halverstadt, *Managing Church Conflict*, 32.

10. Steinke, *How Your Church Family Works*, 106-07; Steinke, *Healthy Congregations* (Bethesda, Md.: Alban, 1996), 27-28; Friedman, *Generation to Generation*, 203-04.

11. Friedman, *Generation to Generation,* 204.

12. Conrad W. Weiser, *Healers–Harmed and Harmful* (Minneapolis: Fortress, 1994), 2, 10.

13. Thomas Merton, *New Seeds of Contemplation* (New York: New Directions, 1961), 72.

14. Stevens and Collins, *Equipping Pastor*, 8.

15. Harriet Goldhor Lerner, *The Dance of Anger* (New York: Harper, 1985), 14-15.

16. Charles H. Cosgrove and Dennis D. Hatfield, *Church Conflict* (Nashville: Abingdon, 1994), 21.

Chapter 3

1. E. Mansell Pattison, *Pastor and Parish* (Philadelphia: Fortress, 1977), 71. Much of this section relies on Pattison.

2. Weiser, *Healers,* 135-36.

3. Moe, *Pastor's Survival Manual*, 44.

4. Pattison, *Pastor and Parish*, 76-77.

5. Pattison, *Pastor and Parish*, 78.

6. Wayne E. Oates, *Pastoral Counseling in Social Problems: Extremism, Race, Sex, Divorce* (Philadelphia: Westminster, 1966), 39; John S. Savage, *The Apathetic and Bored Church Member* (Pittsford, N.Y.: LEAD Consultants, 1976), 25-26.

7. Menno H. Epp, *The Pastor's Exit* (Winnipeg: CMBC Publications, 1984), 27-28.

8. Cited in James McMahon, *The Price of Wisdom* (New York: Crossroad, 1996), 27.

9. Annie Dillard, *An American Childhood* (New York: Harper, 1987), 20.

10. Pattison, *Pastor and Parish*, 54-55.

11. Warner White, "Should I Leave? A Letter from One Priest to Another," in Edward A. White (ed.), *Saying Goodbye: A Time of Growth for Congregations and Pastors* (Washington: Alban, 1990), 4.

12. White, "Should I Leave?," 7.

13. Friedman, *Generation to Generation*, 30.

14. *The Fables of Aesop* (New York: Book-of-the-Month Club, 1995),106.

15. These insights and quotations are from Dietrich Bonhoeffer, *Life Together*, trans. John W. Doberstein (San Francisco: Harper, 1954), 25-30.

16. James E. Dittes, *When the People Say No* (New York: Harper, 1979), 59.

17. Roy M. Oswald, *Making Your Church More Inviting* (Bethesda, Md.: Alban, 1992), 6.

18. *The Rule of St. Benedict in English*, ed. Timothy Fry (Collegeville, Minn.: Liturgical Press, 1982), 92-93. Emphasis added.

19. Donald Capps, "Sex in the Parish: Social-Scientific Explanations for Why It Occurs," *Journal of Pastoral Care* (Winter 1993): 350-61.

20. Steinke, *How Your Church Family Works*, 20-21.

21. Steinke, *How Your Church Family Works*, 21; Friedman, *Generation to Generation,* 231.

22. Steinke, *How Your Church Family Works*, 22.

23. Daniel Goleman, *Emotional Intelligence* (New York: Bantam, 1995), 120ff, 251-55.

24. Goleman, *Emotional Intelligence*, 196-99, 207-10, 231, 231-35, 256-57, chapter 13.

25. Halverstadt, *Managing Church Conflict*, 38ff.

26. Pappas, *Pastoral Stress*, 47.

27. Halverstadt, *Managing Church Conflict*, 201.

Chapter 4
1. C. Jeff Woods, *We've Never Done It Like This Before* (Bethesda, Md.: Alban, 1994), 77.

2. M. Scott Peck, *A World Waiting to be Born* (New York: Bantam, 1993), 301-02.

3. Speed B. Leas, *Should the Pastor Be Fired? How to Deal Constructively with Clergy-Lay Conflict* (Washington: Alban, 1980), 21.

4. Leas, *Moving Your Church Through Conflict*, 35-36.

5. Friedman, *Generation to Generation*, 223.

6. Steinke, *How Your Church Family Works*, 22.

7. Leas, *Should the Pastor Be Fired?*, 4.

8. Pattison, *Pastor and Parish*, 79-80.

9. Steinke, *How Your Church Family Works*, 22.

10. Stevens and Collins, *The Equipping Pastor*, 33.

11. Friedman, *Generation to Generation*, 223.

12. Steinke, *How Your Church Family Works*, 65.

13. Steinke, *How Your Church Family Works*, 65.

14. Steinke, *How Your Church Family Works*, 66.

15. Friedman, *Generation to Generation*, 236-37.

16. Gil Rendle, "On Not Fixing the Church: The Illusion of Congregational Happiness," *Congregations* (May-June 1997): 17.

17. Ronald A. Heifetz, *Leadership Without Easy Answers* (Cambridge: Harvard University Press, 1994), 35ff.

18. Steinke, *Healthy Congregations*, 29.

Chapter 5

1. Lois Hole, *I'll Never Marry a Farmer* (St. Albert, Alberta: Hole's, 1998), 25.

2. Weiser, *Healers*, 139, 141.

3. Halverstadt, *Managing Church Conflict*, 38.

4. Halverstadt, *Managing Church Conflict*, 37.

5. Steinke, *Healthy Congregations*, 27ff.

6. Material here, unless otherwise noted, is derived from a Leas paper, "Levels of Conflict and Tension," 1983, distributed at a "Moving Your Church Through Conflict" seminar conducted by Leas in Waterloo, Ontario, June 1997. References to Leas lectures refer to this seminar.

7. This quotation and those following are from Leas, *Moving Your Church Through Conflict*, 35-36.

8. This quotation and those following are from Speed B. Leas, *Leadership and Conflict* (Nashville: Abingdon, 1982), 88-89, 9.

9. Halverstadt, *Managing Church Conflict*, 27; and Virginia Curran Hoffman, *The Codependent Church* (New York: Crossroad, 1991), 18-19.

10. Halverstadt, *Managing Church Conflict*, 105-06.

11. Halverstadt, *Managing Church Conflict*, 82.

12. Halverstadt, *Managing Church Conflict*, 125, 128, 131.

13. "Agreeing and Disagreeing in Love" is available from Peace and Justice Committee, Mennonite Church, P.O. Box 173, Orrville, Ohio 44667, (330) 683-6844; from Commission on Home Ministries, General Conference Mennonite Church, 722 Main Street, P.O. Box 347, Newton, Kans. 67114, (316) 283-5100; or from Faith and Life Press Canada, 600 Shaftesbury Blvd., Winnipeg, Manitoba R3P 0M4, (204) 888-6781. (The document is accompanied by brief suggestions about biblical foundations, suggestions for a process of studying and implementing the guidelines, and ways of using the guidelines.)

14. Leas, *Should the Pastor Be Fired?*, 13-14.

15. Friedman, *Generation to Generation*, 50.

16. Friedman, *Generation to Generation*, 79.

Chapter 6

1. Raymond Chandler, *Pearls Are a Nuisance* (New York: Penguin, 1950), 198.

2. Friedman, *Generation to Generation*, 81-82.

3. Oates, *Pastoral Counseling in Social Problems*, 49; *The Care of Troublesome People* (Bethesda, Md.: Alban, 1994), 15.

4. Friedman, *Generation to Generation*, 52-53.

5. Speed B. Leas, *A Lay Person's Guide to Conflict Management* (Washington: Alban, 1979), 6; Leas, *Should the Pastor Be Fired?*, 13.

6. Steinke, *Healthy Congregations*, 54ff; Steinke, *How Your Church Family Works*, 24-25.

7. Steinke, *Healthy Congregations*, 40.

8. Steinke, *Healthy Congregations*, 58-59.

9. John Howard Yoder, *He Came Preaching Peace* (Scottdale, Pa.: Herald Press, 1985), 120.

10. John Howard Yoder, *The Royal Priesthood* (Grand Rapids: Eerdmans, 1994), 122.

11. Leas, *Should the Pastor Be Fired?*, 4; Leas, *Moving Your Church Through Conflict*, 36; Epp, *Pastor's Exit*, 60.

12. Yoder, *Royal Priesthood*, 335-36. For more information on God's purposes of restitution and reconciliation, particularly in criminal justice issues, see chapters 3-5 of Arthur Paul Boers, *Justice that Heals* (Newton, Kans.: Faith and Life Press, 1992).

13. Yoder, *Royal Priesthood*, 343-44.

14. Leas, *Should the Pastor Be Fired?*, 3.

15. Daniel G. Bagby, *Understanding Anger in the Church* (Nashville: Broadman, 1979), 142.

Chapter 7

1. Halverstadt, *Managing Church Conflict*, 46.

2. Steinke, *Healthy Congregations*, 99.

3. Friedman, *Generation to Generation*, 220-21.

4. Friedman, *Generation to Generation*, 198.

5. Friedman, *Generation to Generation*, 30.

6. Friedman, *Generation to Generation*, 249.

7. Epp, *Pastor's Exit*, 24.

8. Friedman, *Generation to Generation*, 83.

9. Friedman, *Generation to Generation*, 82.

10. Ronald W. Richardson, *Creating a Healthier Church* (Minneapolis: Fortress, 1996), 181.

11. Goleman, *Emotional Intelligence*, 16.

12. Steinke, *How Your Church Family Works*, 18.

13. Goleman, *Emotional Intelligence*, 26, 48; Steinke, *How Your Church Family Works*, 17, 107-08.

14. Steinke, *How Your Church Family Works*, 72.

15. Richardson, *Creating a Healthier Church*, 42.

16. Steinke, *How Your Church Family Works*, 14.

17. Steinke, *How Your Church Family Works*, 20.

18. Friedman, *Generation to Generation*, 208-09.

19. Friedman, *Generation to Generation*, 210.

20. Leas, *Leadership and Conflict*, 61-62.

21. John A. Coil, "Yes, But How Do I Become a Nonanxious Presence?," *Congregations* (November-December 1994): 14-16.

22. Richardson, *Creating a Healthier Church*, 178-80.

23. Goleman, *Emotional Intelligence*, 34.

24. Palmer, *Courage to Teach*, 57.

25. Metropolitan Anthony, *Courage to Pray*, trans. Dinah Livingstone (Crestwood, N.Y.: St. Vladimir's Press, 1984), 30ff.

Chapter 8

1. Belden Lane, *The Solace of Fierce Landscapes* (New York: Oxford University Press, 1998), 136.

2. Peck, *World Waiting to Be Born*, 357.

3. Friedman, *Generation to Generation*, 148.

4. Heifetz, *Leadership Without Easy Answers*, 5.

5. Heifetz, *Leadership Without Easy Answers*, 183.

6. Epp, *Pastor's Exit,* 28; Leas's study of terminated pastors also saw defensive behavior as a common professional and ethical problem among involuntarily terminated pastors (*Should the Pastor Be Fired?*, 21).

7. Dittes, *When the People Say No*, 144-45.

8. Heifetz, *Leadership Without Easy Answers*, 263.

9. Garret Keizer, *A Dresser of Sycamore Trees* (San Francisco: Harper & Row, 1991), 66.

10. Steinke, *How Your Church Family Works*, 88-89.

11. Leas, *Leadership and Conflict*, 117.

12. John Savage, *Listening and Caring Skills in Ministry* (Nashville: Abingdon, 1996), 57, 66.

13. Leas, *Leadership and Conflict*, 115-19.

14. Leas, *Leadership and Conflict*, 117.

15. Savage, *Listening and Caring Skills in Ministry*, 63.

16. Norma Cole McKinnon, "Making and Taking Criticism," *Practice of Ministry in Canada* (November 1994): 28-29.

17. James A. Sparks, "When Criticism Comes: Understanding and Working Through Our Defensiveness," *Congregations* (November-December 1997): 7.

18. Alan C. Filley, *Interpersonal Conflict Resolution* (Dallas: Scott, Foresman, 1975), 42.

19. Leas, *Should the Pastor Be Fired?*, 22.

20. Leas, *Should the Pastor Be Fired?*, 20.

21. Dittes, *When the People Say No*, 59.

22. Henri J. M. Nouwen, *Reaching Out* (Garden City, N.Y.: Doubleday, 1975), 36.

23. Nouwen, *Reaching Out*, 37.

24. Friedman, *Generation to Generation,* 46.

25. Christina Feldman and Jack Kornfield, *Stories of the Spirit, Stories of the Heart* (San Francisco: Harper, 1991), 56.

26. Parker Palmer, *The Promise of Paradox* (Notre Dame, Ind.: Ave Maria, 1980), 82.

27. Henri J. M. Nouwen, *The Road to Peace*, ed. John Dear (Maryknoll, N.Y.: Orbis, 1998), 171.

28. Friedman, *Generation to Generation*, 10.

Chapter 9

1. Leas, *Should the Pastor Be Fired?*, 9.

2. Timothy E. O'Connell, *Making Disciples* (New York: Crossroad, 1998), 108.

3. Goleman, *Emotional Intelligence*, 43, 80ff.

4. Heifetz, *Leadership Without Easy Answers*, 271-72.

5. Savage, *The Apathetic and Bored Church Member*, 68-69.

6. Bagby, *Understanding Anger*, 40.

7. Bagby, *Understanding Anger*, 142.

8. Leas, *Should the Pastor Be Fired?*, 5ff.

9. Friedman, *Generation to Generation*, 211-12.

10. Heifetz, *Leadership Without Easy Answers*, 68.

11. Heifetz, *Leadership Without Easy Answers*, 273.

12. Heifetz, *Leadership Without Easy Answers*, 273.

CONFLICT

Bagby, Daniel G. *Understanding Anger in the Church*. Nashville: Broadman, 1979.

Dittes, James E. *When the People Say No: Conflict and the Call to Ministry*. New York: Harper, 1979.

Filley, Alan C. *Interpersonal Conflict Resolution*. Dallas: Scott, Foresman, 1975.

Halverstadt, Hugh F. *Managing Church Conflict*. Louisville: Westminster John Knox, 1991.

Leas, Speed B. *A Lay Person's Guide to Conflict Management*. Washington: Alban, 1979.

———. *Leadership and Conflict*. Nashville: Abingdon, 1982.

———. *Moving Your Church Through Conflict*. Washington: Alban, 1985.

Smith, Donald P. *Clergy in the Cross Fire: Coping with Role Conflicts in the Ministry*. Philadelphia: Westminster, 1973.

Willimon, William H. *Preaching About Conflict in the Local Church*. Philadelphia: Westminster, 1987.

DIFFICULT BEHAVIOR

Bramson, Robert M. *Coping with Difficult People*. New York: Doubleday, 1981.

Brinkman, Rick, and Rick Kirschner. *Dealing With People You Can't Stand: How to Bring Out the Best in People at Their Worst*. New York: McGraw-Hill, 1994.

Dale, Robert D. *Surviving Difficult Church Members*. Nashville: Abingdon, 1984.

Ellis, Albert, and Arthur Lange. *How to Keep People from Pushing Your Buttons*. New York: Birch Lane Press, 1994.

Haugk, Kenneth C. *Antagonists in the Church: How to Identify and Deal with Destructive Conflict*. Minneapolis: Augsburg, 1988.

Oates, Wayne E. *Behind the Masks: Personality Disorders in Religious Behavior*. Louisville: Westminster, 1987.

———. *The Care of Troublesome People*. Bethesda, Md.: Alban, 1994.

———. *Pastoral Counseling in Social Problems: Extremism, Race, Sex, Divorce*. Philadelphia: Westminster, 1966.

Rediger, G. Lloyd. *Clergy Killers: Guidance for Pastors and Congregations Under Attack*. Inver Grove Heights, Minn.: Logos Productions, 1997.

Savage, John S. *The Apathetic and Bored Church Member*. Pittsford, N.Y.: LEAD Consultants, 1976.

Segal, Judith. *Dealing with Difficult Men*. New York: Harper, 1993.

Shelley, Marshall. *Well-Intentioned Dragons: Ministering to Problem People in the Church*. Minneapolis: Bethany House, 1985.

FAMILY SYSTEMS THEORY AND UNDERSTANDING CHURCH STRUCTURES

Cosgrove, Charles H., and Dennis D. Hatfield. *Church Conflict: The Hidden Systems Behind the Fights*. Nashville: Abingdon, 1994.

Friedman, Edwin H. *Generation to Generation: Family Process in Church and Synagogue*. New York: Guilford Press, 1985.

Hoffman, Virginia Curran. *The Codependent Church*. New York: Crossroad, 1991.

Lerner, Harriet Goldhor. *The Dance of Anger*. New York: Harper, 1985.

Pattison, E. Mansell. *Pastor and Parish: A Systems Approach*. Philadelphia: Fortress, 1977.

Richardson, Ronald W. *Creating a Healthier Church: Family Systems Theory, Leadership, and Congregational Life*. Minneapolis: Fortress, 1996.

Steinke, Peter L. *Healthy Congregations: A Systems Approach*. Bethesda: Alban, 1996.

————. *How Your Church Family Works: Understanding Congregations as Emotional Systems*. Bethesda: Alban, 1993.

Stevens, R. Paul, and Phil Collins. *The Equipping Pastor*. Bethesda, Md.: Alban, 1993.

LEADERSHIP AND PASTORAL CARE

Capps, Donald. "Sex in the Parish: Social-Scientific Explanations for Why It Occurs." *Journal of Pastoral Care* (Winter 1993): 350-61.

Coil, John A. "Yes, But *How* Do I Become a Nonanxious Presence?" *Congregations* (November-December 1994): 14-16.

Covey, Stephen R. *The Seven Habits of Highly Effective People: Powerful Lessons in Personal Change*. New York: Simon & Schuster, 1989.

Heifetz, Ronald A. *Leadership Without Easy Answers*. Cambridge: Harvard University Press, 1994.

McKinnon, Norma Cole. "Making and Taking Criticism." *Practice of Ministry in Canada* (November 1994): 27-29.

Moe, Kenneth Alan. *The Pastor's Survival Manual: Ten Perils in Parish Ministry and How to Handle Them*. Bethesda, Md.: Alban, 1995.

Pappas, Anthony G. *Pastoral Stress: Sources of Tension, Resources for Transformation*. Bethesda, Md.: Alban, 1995.

Rendle, Gil. "On Not Fixing the Church: The Illusion of Congregational Happiness." *Congregations* (May-June, 1997): 15-17.

Savage, John. *Listening and Caring Skills in Ministry: A Guide for Pastors, Counselors, and Small Group Leaders*. Nashville: Abingdon, 1996.
Sparks, James A. "When Criticism Comes: Understanding and Working Through Our Defensiveness." *Congregations* (November-December 1997): 5-7.
Underwood, Ralph L. *Empathy and Confrontation in Pastoral Care*. Philadelphia: Fortress, 1985.
Weiser, Conrad W. *Healers—Harmed and Harmful*. Minneapolis: Fortress, 1994.
White, Warner. "Should I Leave? A Letter from One Priest to Another." In Edward A. White (ed.), *Saying Goodbye: A Time of Growth for Congregations and Pastors*. Washington: Alban, 1990, 3-14.
Woods, C. Jeff. *We've Never Done It Like This Before*. Bethesda, Md.: Alban, 1994.

PASTORAL TERMINATIONS
Epp, Menno H. *The Pastor's Exit*. Winnipeg: CMBC Publications, 1984.
Leas, Speed B. *Should the Pastor Be Fired? How to Deal Constructively with Clergy-Lay Conflict*. Washington: Alban, 1980.
Smith, Michael. "Pastors Under Fire: A Personal Report." *Christian Century* (23 February 1994): 196-98.

PSYCHOLOGICAL
Goleman, Daniel. *Emotional Intelligence: Why It Can Matter More Than IQ*. New York: Bantam, 1995.
McMahon, James. *The Price of Wisdom*. New York: Crossroad, 1996.
Peck, M. Scott. *A World Waiting to Be Born: Civility Rediscovered*. New York: Bantam, 1993.

THEOLOGY AND SPIRITUALITY
Anthony, Metropolitan, *Courage to Pray* (Dinah Livingstone, trans.). Crestwood, N.Y.: St. Vladimir's Press, 1984.
Bonhoeffer, Dietrich. *Life Together* (John W. Doberstein, trans.). San Francisco: Harper, 1954.
O'Connell, Timothy E. *Making Disciples*. New York: Crossroad, 1998.
Palmer, Parker J. *The Promise of Paradox*. Notre Dame, Ind.: Ave Maria, 1980.
Yoder, John Howard. *He Came Preaching Peace*. Scottdale, Pa.: Herald Press, 1985.
———. *The Royal Priesthood*. Grand Rapids: Eerdmans, 1994.